Port Vale FC

The Valiants in the 50s & 60s

Introduction

Fans who were present during the Fifties and Sixties witnessed some of the Valiants more dramatic changes of fortune. It was a period of time that saw some of Port Vale's most talented players and startling matches.

Vale also managed to lure gifted managers who made their own unique imprint in the club's history.

At the start of the Fifties the club underwent a change of venue – they left their old ground in Hanley to move to Vale Park, Burslem. The inaugural match played on 24 August 1950 saw a club record crowd of 30,042 turn up to watch Vale beat Newport County 1-0.

Vale continued to grow in strength under the management of ex-Stoke City player Freddie Steele. He made Vale famous for its 'Iron Curtain' defence which was the lynch-pin for Vale's exciting 1954 FA Cup run.

Norman Low took over as manager for Vale in 1957 after Steele resigned. The team had slipped to the bottom of the Second Division and unfortunately Low couldn't halt their further decline into the 'new' Fourth Division by the end of the 1958-59 season.

The Sixties are marked by the arrivals and departures of Port Vale managers. Although Vale had glimmers of brilliance they slipped further and further down in the divsions.

The return of Freddie Steele to Vale in 1962 failed to see Valiants rise to the heights they had achieved under his management in the 1950s. He was replaced as manager in 1965 by another ex-Stoke City player, Jackie Mudie, who, in turn, was replaced in 1967 by the legendary Sir Stanley Matthews. Matthews was still manager when Vale were expelled from the Football League in 1968 for 'money irregularities' and fined the sum of £4,000. Shortly after Matthews resigned as manager.

It was under Gordon Lee's dedicated management that Vale finally saw promotion from the Fourth Division at the end of the 1969-70 season.

The images in this book have been gathered together from The Sentinel's photographic archives, many of these photographs have never previously been published. We have also selected some of the match reports and articles written by The Sentinel's reporters and guest writers, like Roy Sproson, to include in this book. While this book is not a definitive source for Vale in this time period we hope that it will renew fond memories and provide a unique glimpse into Port Vale's incredible history.

Contents

Chapter One
1950-1953

The early Fifties witnessed many changes at Port Vale – including a change of venue from the Old Recreation Ground in Hanley to the new stadium in Burslem. Vale's Walter Aveyard was the first man to score a goal at the new ground in a match against Newport County where Vale won 1-0.

South African Gordon Hodgson was the manager for Vale at the time of the move, he maintained Port Vale's comfortable position in the middle of Third Division (South). Tragically he died at the age of 47 from cancer and as Ray King writes in the article featured later in this chapter, Hodgson '...could not do enough for his players.'

Ivor Powell briefly succeeded Hodgson, but Powell was replaced six months later by one of Vale's most successful and well-loved managers, Freddie Steele. Steele was an ex-Stoke City and England International player and he signed for Vale as player-manager in 1951. It wasn't long before Steele retired from playing to concentrate on the management of Port Vale.

In the 1952-53 season Vale secured their place at the top of the Third Division (North), finishing only one point behind leaders Oldham. By this stage Port Vale were known for their strong defensive play and a first team side that were ready to take on some of the best teams in the country. Freddie Steele had forged a formidable side.

In the final stages of demolition is the Old Recreation Ground in Hanley. This was home to the Valiants for many years but in August 1950 Port Vale made the move to the new Burslem ground. The old stadium and pitch were destroyed and a municipal car park was built on the site.

Luck was too good to last
By Ray King

It all began for me in a remote part of North Northumbria, where there was little or nothing to do.

The usual thing for children was to kick a stone around in the road, play in the local park until it was dark and only dream of the day when the chance might come along of playing for one of the famous local teams. Newcastle United or Sunderland, 30 miles and 40 miles away, respectively.

In 1942 my mother had just brought me a new pair of boots. They were green and the best I ever had. I was playing in goal for my local team, Amble. All league football had been suspended and all matches were played as friendlies on Sundays.

It therefore came as a big surprise when there was a knock on our door one Friday evening. The manager of the local team told me Newcastle wanted me to play the following day for their reserves at St James Park. The previous week I had been there to watch England play Scotland in a wartime international, so to play on that same pitch seemed too good to be true.

Before the game I had never experienced the sort of nerves I was to endure for the rest of my football career. I even had a nose bleed. Once on the park though all nerves are gone; at least, most of them.

I only had two games in the reserves and had reached the age of 17 when United signed me as a professional. The following week I had an even greater thrill when I was selected to play in the first team against Sunderland at St James Park.

The Sunderland team at that time had great players like Hastings, Duns, Carter and Burbanks. I had only read about them and had a tremendous feeling of awe just to hear their names mentioned. I cannot remember much about the game except the result was 2-2. I could not have done too badly because I kept my place for quite some time.

More excitement was to come for me. After playing against Manchester City, who included the great Frank Swift and Peter Doherty, Frank told a newspaper reporter that I was the best keeper he had seen at such a young age, but thought I was a bit too confident.

Perhaps by that he meant the way I went out for high crosses and caught them one-handed. I never wore gloves, even with a greasy ball. I can only put it down to arrogance of youth.

Further to that, the managing director of Newcastle, Stan Seymour, told me that I would be United's No. 1 keeper when League football started up again after the war.

PERHAPS IT WOULD BE AN UNDERSTATEMENT TO SAY I WAS ON CLOUD NINE AND EVEN AT SUCH A YOUNG AGE I KNEW THIS SORT OF LUCK COULD NOT LAST.

I did not have to wait long to realise that.

Soon after reaching the age of 18 I was called up into the Army, in which I was to serve four and a half years. It can be said I was lucky not to be sent to any danger zones during that time, but from a footballing point of view my luck had certainly ended.

Chester signed me as wartime guest player. For 10 or 12 games all went well until, when playing at Goodison Park against Everton, I saved a penalty from Tommy Lawton (then at the peak of his career) and broke the scavoid in my right wrist.

This was the start of an alarming run of injuries for me. During Army games I had my left wrist and right thumb broken, plus sinovitis of the knee, which put me in hospital for nine weeks. A lot of the time I played outside-right and centre-forward and became quite proficient. I am sure it is a bigger thrill scoring than making brilliant saves.

In 1945-46 season, Newcastle United asked me to play for them again, even though I was right off goalkeeping practice. Mind you I did not tell them that. At the time Newcastle had a fine side, with players like Bobby Cowell, Joe Harvey, Jackie Milburn, Ernie Taylor, Albert Stubbins and Charlie Wayman. Teaming up with them was a great thrill and I went on to play 40-odd games before my luck ran out again.

Playing at Bradford, when their team included Len Shackleton, I happened to punch the crossbar, resulting in terrific pain. Trainers at

that time knew nothing about injuries and this particular sponge man tried to assure me it was only a sprain. For 12 more games I carried on with increasing pain, my confidence gradually leaving me.

With 60,000-65,000 spectators at St James Park at that time, most of them were bound to notice and quite a few let me know in no uncertain terms that it was time for me to go. My last game was against Bolton Wanderers. The previous week had been the Bolton V. Stoke disaster match, when more than 30 people died. Nat Lofthouse was in the team and just making his name. We lost 3-2 and I felt partly to blame.

After the game I demanded that I be taken to hospital for an X-ray. It proved positive. I spent another nine months in plaster.

In 1947, while stationed near London, I was signed by Leyton Orient on a temporary transfer, my first game being away to Northampton in the Third Division, League football having resumed. During the second half, while diving to punch the ball away, my wrist was broken again. I felt this was the end of the road. Six weeks later I decided to have a run-out in their reserve side against Charlton. My wrist went again when I was just catching an innocuous ball.

Until I was demobbed in 1947, goalkeeping was out and I just played outfield for Amble in the Northern Alliance. Newcastle were still interested, however, and asked if I would play in goal again, so that they could watch me. This I did and in diving at a player's feet I was kicked on the jaw, breaking it in two places. End of United's interest! I was only 22 years of age, but it seemed I had lived a lifetime and here I was on the scrapheap. For two years I did not play in goal until Ashington, of the North-Eastern League, asked me to give it another try.

Eventually I agreed to do so (it is true goalkeepers are mad) and I played in several games without much conviction. That was until I played at Roker Park against Sunderland Reserves. Just being in that atmosphere again gave me the incentive to get back.

I could now see light at the end of the tunnel and felt that if I did not make the effort to get back into League football at this point I would never make it. As it happened my brother, George, who had started his career with Newcastle as a centre-forward and then moved on to Hull, had just been transferred to Port Vale.

He happened to mention me to the manager at the time, Gordon Hodgson, and he invited me to play in the final of the Staffordshire Senior Cup against Walsall.

My first impression of the Recreation Ground, Hanley, was one of amazement. I really thought I had landed in Tobago or some shanty town way out West. The stands, such as they were, looked as though one gust of wind would blow the lot down. The dressing-rooms resembled a dungeon, but it may seem strange to say that I felt completely at home.

I SPENT MY FIRST YEAR BACK IN FOOTBALL AS A VERY HAPPY MAN

Mr Hodgson was a South African. He had played as a centre-forward with Liverpool and England and he had also been a fast bowler with Lancashire. An enormous man of 6ft 3in., he always wore a large trilby hat, with an even larger brim. He was indeed an imposing figure.

The trainer, Ken Fish, was also South African. He had played centre-forward with Aston Villa, although never hitting the high spots. He, too, was well over 6ft. tall and had the build to go with it. His assistant trainer was the late Bill Cope, who in his day had been a strong, aggressive wing-half with Bolton. Bill was a gruff, down-to-earth character and stood no nonsense from anyone.

The Walsall game is one I shall never forget. Fast and furious from the start, it was most enjoyable, but I was amazed at the high standard. Several of the Vale players were as good as I had seen anywhere. We won 1-0 the goal coming from Stan Polk, who scored with a tremendous drive. It was especially wonderful for me to keep a clean sheet, come through unscathed and receive a medal in the bargain.

Perhaps the one blot was the fact that Ray Hancock, one of the other keepers, had played in the previous rounds and I know very well how disappointed he must have been.

As it happened I found Ray to be a most delightful lad, with an enormous wit. He often had us all in stitches. The other keeper was George Heppell. He also came from the North-East of England and had been regular keeper for many years. George was a great favourite with the crowd, popular with the players and rightly so, as I found him also a smashing chap.

This of course, made it more difficult for me as an intruder, but over the years, although competing for the same position, I cannot ever remember a cross word between us.

At right-back in the Walsall game was a slightly-built lad called Jim Elsby and what a display he gave. Apparently he was being talked about as a star of the future and on that display he looked it. Sadly Jim received a knee injury shortly afterwards and never really got over it.

Luck does play an enormous part in football, like everything else, and I always remember Stan Seymour saying that football was five per cent skill, 15 per cent guts and 80 per cent luck. Perhaps he was not too far wrong.

That team included Garth Butler, at left-back. He was part-time and came from Derby. A most unlikely looking footballer, he was a mass of nerves before the game, although he had been a regular for several seasons. He used to take several different coloured pills before each game. They must have done the trick, for as soon as he got on the pitch he was completely transformed. The crowd called him the "assassin."

At right-half was Norman Hallam, a man of the cloth. Nobody swore when Norman was around. To see him play, no-one would have guessed his other profession. He was strong in the tackle and had a fair amount of skill. Tommy Cheadle, at centre-half, I have already written about.

Bill McGarry, at left-half, gave the best display I ever saw from any wing-half. Strange to say, as far as I know he never played again at left-half, always on the right side.

At outside-right was Ronnie Allen, probably the best two-footed player in the game.

RONNIE AND I WOULD OFTEN GO BACK TO THE GROUND IN THE AFTERNOON SO THAT HE COULD PRACTICE HIS PENALTY KICKS WITH BOTH FEET. IT WAS IRONIC THAT I SHOULD HAVE TO FACE HIM AGAIN IN THE F.A. CUP SEMI-FINAL

At inside-right was Alan Martin another local discovery, who later went to Stoke City. At centre-forward was my brother, George King, whose main ability was in the air. Very fast inside-left was Stan Polk, who along with Micky Hulligan, from Liverpool, completed an excellent side.

At the start of the 1949-50 season I was first-team choice, although my wrists were heavily strapped by Ken Fish before each game. It seemed as though I had never been out of the game and my confidence had completely returned. We were riding high in the Third Division and the scouts were flocking to each match, mainly to watch Ronnie Allen and Bill McGarry.

Our team talks were practically nil. In fact, they were a real education. Gordon Hodgson would come into the dressing-room just before kick-off, stand with legs apart, hat on the back of his head and says: "Cor blimey lads, surely you can beat this bloody lot."

For all Gordon's shortcomings as a coach, he was a marvellous man and could not do enough for the players. We were treated like a First Division side, stopping for meals at the best restaurants and overnight travel even to London, staying in the best hotels.

A lot of talk at the time was about the new ground being constructed in Burslem for the following season. It was to be the 'Wembley of the North' and, of course everyone was excited at the prospect of playing there.

31 March 1984

Although this picture is taken in the late 1940s, Walter Aveyard played for Port Vale from 1948-1952. In total he made 108 appearances for Vale as centre-forward and scored 29 goals. Among many things Aveyard will be remembered as the first player to score a goal at Vale Park.

Vale pose for the camera before the start of their last game at the Old Recreation Ground.

Top scorer for Port Vale in 1951-52 was none other than Cliff Pinchbeck. He scored 20 League and Cup goals for Vale. Eventually he moved clubs to Northampton Town.

Pictured here are some of Port Vale's directors. Seated: Flint, Holdcroft, Diffen. Stood behind, Hollus, Cooper, Burgess, Dodson.

Fans I could never forget

We had just missed promotion the previous season. Ronnie Allen had been transferred to West Bromwich for a large fee and several changes were being made on the playing side.

Lol Hamlett had been signed from Bolton to play at right-back, even though he had spent most of his career as a centre-half. His experience was to prove invaluable. My brother had moved to Barrow and Cliff Pinchbeck, a big strapping chap from Everton, was signed to replace him.

Vale Park was opened for the first match of the season and with a crowd of 30,042. I must say it was most impressive. What a contrast to the Old Recreation Ground! Lovely large dressing-rooms, but there was only a small cover over the directors' stand. The rest was all open terracing.

We won the game (against Newport) 1-0, so everyone was happy. Unfortunately happiness never lasts long. Results were fluctuating and there were problems off the pitch. Gordon Hodgson seemed to get very depressed and events were not turning out very well for me either.

First of all I received notification from the Army that I had to report to Salisbury Plain for two weeks' Z-training. This meant I was going to miss a couple of games. At least the manager was very sympathetic and assured me my first team place was secure when I returned.

What a shock it was to find on my return that Gordon Hodgson had died and was already buried. Apparently, he had been suffering from cancer for some time, but none of us knew. We were all very saddened. He was not only our manager, but also a good friend.

Ken Fish was in temporary charge of the side until a new manager was appointed and he decided to keep George Heppell in goal. Naturally I was disappointed, but George had apparently played well and I accepted the situation. Perhaps I may not have accepted it quite so well if I had known the outcome, although I did manage to get back into the side for a couple of games. They were to be my last for a very long time.

One of the games is worth recording. It was against Crystal Palace at home. The pitch had started to cut up badly and we completely overran Palace. Our young reserve Len Barber was playing centre-forward and he gave an amazing display in the mud, scoring six goals before the game was called off. The pitch had deteriorated so much.

It did seem a shame, with it being a wonderful achievement. Len was only a slip of a lad, but he just floated over the mud.

A new player-manager was appointed, Ivor Powell, from Aston Villa, where he had found fame as a Welsh international wing-half. From the very start he appeared to take a dislike to me and this was borne out by the fact that I did not have one first-team game with him in charge.

Before Ivor Powell arrived the team were just holding their own as a middle-of-the-table side, but it was a continual deterioration and his own displays were really dreadful. He had the most wonderful vocabulary and in his best Welsh voice he used words that no-one had ever heard. His favourite words, though, were to "har-ass the opposition."

He brought about his own downfall by trying to rule by fear. The team were now rock-bottom and the directors called the players one by one into the Boardroom to get their opinion of the manager.

It was quite pathetic to see Ivor Powell going up to each player pleading with him to put in a good word. The outcome was inevitable. Mr Powell was sacked the following day and I have never known such a change in atmosphere in the dressing-room: complete relief.

A new appointment had to be made quickly if the team were to have any chance of getting away from the bottom rung. It turned out to be a very popular choice in Freddie Steele, the former Stoke City and England centre-forward, who had been player-manager at Mansfield.

Freddie Steele did a fine job from the start and the team began to pick up and soon got away from the foot of the table. I had not seen Freddie play before, but in one particular game against Plymouth he gave the best display I had ever seen at centre-forward and I had played against the best in Lawton, Ford, Charles, Lofthouse, Liddell. None could have bettered him that day.

Off the field he was a difficult man to get to know and I found him a bit of an enigma. I will say this though: he had the most marvellous way of getting players to pull out all the stops for him and, but for a suspect temperament, I reckon he could have been a top manager for a very long time. I will deal with that temperament later.

George Heppell had left the club and Ray Hancock and I were competing for the first-team position. We continued to be good friends and both loved playing outfield in practice games. It was always a battle to see who could get most goals. Bill McGarry used to say I only had one trick, but I still beat him with it.

During the 1951-52 season I was in the first team when we had to play away to Bradford City. Ivor Powell had been appointed manager and my brother had been signed from Barrow. Inevitably there was a lot of speculation about the

game and the Press gave it good coverage. The score was 0-0 with only 10 minutes to go when my brother beat me with a glancing header, much to his and the team's delight. Freddie Steele nearly went berserk. He accused me of giving the goal away on purpose and that I had connived with my brother.

I treated his remarks with the contempt they deserved, but it upset me dreadfully. Ivor Powell was, of course jubilant at having beaten his old club, but taking me to one side, he apologised for the way he had treated me at Vale Park.

Apparently the chairman, Mr Holdcroft, had given Ivor Powell strict instructions not to play me in the first team at any price. This rang a bell with me right away. During my first season at Vale I happened to get married. Shortly afterwards Mr Holdcroft told me that he had acquired a house for me to buy and had actually arranged the date for us to move in. He told me he could not get the key for this particular house, but showed me around the one next door, which he had lived in previously. He said it was exactly the same as the one he had purchased on our behalf.

So here we were moving into a house we had never seen. The day we moved in was freezing cold and on opening the front door floods of water were cascading down the stairs from burst pipes. It was a heartbreaking start for us, especially when we found the house in a great need of repair. We could only suffer it for a short while and decided we had to get out and we spent a considerable time in digs. The chairman was livid and never forgave me. Worse was to come following the Bradford City match.

Freddie Steele had organised a practice match on the Tuesday morning and he relegated me to the reserves. He was playing against me in the first team and what happened I shall never forget as long as I live.

A long through ball came straight to me with no-one in attendance. As I picked up the ball Freddie came rushing up, had a tremendous lunge as if to kick the ball out of my hands and succeeded in splitting the webbing of my fingers wide open. I went straight to hospital, where they inserted 12 stitches. I had only recently recovered from a similar injury and had been playing most of the season with my middle fingers strapped together.

This latest injury happened near the end of the season and I did not play again. Nor indeed did I play one first-team game the following season in 1952-53, and yet I can honestly say that my form was the best I had ever produced.

To be fair, the first team were having a great season and Ray Hancock had been performing well. They just missed out on promotion.

During that particular close season I was determined to get into that team, so to toughen myself up I took a job as a labourer on a building site. Although I found it hard work, I really enjoyed it and had never felt so strong and fit for a very long time.

The pre-season games were Probables v. Possibles. I played in goal for the Possibles and I cannot ever remember having played so well in a practice game. I was fighting for my life and the Possibles won 4-2, which really put the cat among the pigeons.

Come the day before the first game of the season and all the players were in the dressing-room waiting for the team-sheet to be put up by the manager. When Freddie came through the door he looked me straight in the eye, then I knew there was no need to look for my name. I was in.

I have told you of the culmination of my time at Vale Park, but looking back I know I will never forget the welcome the Potteries people gave me from the start. Of course, I had my critics, but on the whole my eight years with Vale were happy and I have so much for

which to thank the people. I even had my own little fan club, which kept going for several years. They followed my progress wherever I went in football and kept me in touch with affairs at the Vale.

It was particularly flattering to me at the time Stoke City signed Gordon Banks from Leicester. They wrote "Stoke have Banks, but we had the King." Can anyone have better support than that?

I cannot end these reminiscences without mentioning some of the fine young players who were at the Vale during my time.

Alan Bennett at outside-left had all the hallmarks of a top-class player, but like Jim Elsby he was cruelly struck down by injury. There was John Poole, a fine goalkeeper, Bernard Finney, Derek Mountford, Derek Tomkinson, who deputised for Ken Griffiths in the F.A. Cup semi-final, Terry Austin, John Abbotts, Tommy Conway, Stan Smith, Terry Bullivant and Stan Steele. Some of them made many first-team appearances and there were so many more. I can see faces, but the names elude me.

I must not forget dear Jimmy Todd, the Irish lad who came from Blackpool. He was a marvellous competitor. A special mention, too, for the great Neil Franklin, who trained with us on occasions and helped me with special ball skill training.

No-one can have had more ups and downs than I had, but one must never give up. Football is the greatest game in the world. It was spoiled on occasions by the people who ran the clubs. We did enjoy our football, even though there was not much money, but we have our memories.

I often talk to Peter Shilton when he comes to the beach here in Poole. He earns approximately £3,000 a week, but he does not seem to be any happier than I was with £17 a week.

Footballers are all a bit vain. They love the limelight, love to be praised and resent criticism. With my arthritic back and wrists, the legacy of shoulder charges and broken bones, I often wonder whether it was all worthwhile. Of course it was. I would do it all again. I only hope I would have more commonsense. It saddens me to see the team still struggling in the lower reaches of the Third Division. One day though they will rise again. Like vintage wine, how can they fail with a name like Port Vale?

7 April 1984

Alderman William Holdcroft was instrumental in Port Vale's move from the old ground in Hanley to the new Vale Park in Burslem. He began his working life at the age of 12 as a pit boy. Holdcroft went on to establish a musical instrument and furniture business and became Lord Mayor of Stoke-on-Trent in 1939. He became chairman to Port Vale in July 1946 and remained until 1952. Holdcroft returned in 1954 as the Club President but sadly died the following year.

Reg Potts played his first game for Port Vale in 1945 but his football career was interrupted by National Service. By the early 1950s he was a regular first team player and was a key member of the FA Cup run team in 1954. He played his last game for Vale in 1957 in a derby match against Stoke City.

Ivor Powell's stay at Vale was somewhat short lived. The former Queen's Park Rangers, Aston Villa and Welsh international joined Vale as player-manager during the summer of 1951 as a replacement for Gordon Hodgson who had sadly died aged just 47. However Powell was only six months into the job when his contract was terminated due to Vale's lacklustre form.

Arriving at Stamford Bridge to see Vale's cup opponents, Chelsea play West Bromwich Albion are (left to right): Mr F W Burgess, Alderman W A Holdcroft (two of Vale's directors) and Mr Freddie Steele, Port Vale's manager.

Tom Cheadle made a total of 358 League and Cup appearances for Vale and was captain during the club's vital 1953-54 season.

Basil Haywood set a club record during the 1952-53 season when he scored in seven consecutive League games. He scored twice in Vale's 4-1 away win at Crewe Alexandra. When Crewe came to Vale the following week Haywood scored twice again. He then followed this by scoring in each of the games against Rochdale, Darlington, Gateshead and Scunthorpe United and finished his run with two goals against Hartlepool United.

Vale legend Ronnie Allen played 135 League and Cup games for the club before being transferred to West Bromwich Albion for £20,000 in March 1950.

Selwyn Whalley joined Vale in August 1953 and made his debut as right-half against Bristol Rovers. He became a part-time player in 1957 after accepting a teaching post at Hanley High School and eventually retired in 1966 due to injury.

Port Vale squad. Back row, from left to right: Albert Mullard, Stan Turner, Roy Sproson, Ray King, Basil Haywood, Reg Potts. Middle row: Ken Fish (trainer), Colin Askey, Albert Leake, Tom Cheadle, Ken Griffiths, Dickie Cunliff, Freddie Steele. Front row: Mick Hulligan, unknown, Jimmy Elds, Alan Bennett.

Mr Fred Steele – Manager of Port Vale

Mr Fred Steele, the former England and Stoke City centre-forward, who was appointed Player-Manager of Port Vale in December 1951, today signed a three-year contract with the club as Manager.

His last appearance for the Vale as a player may be next Monday evening, when his team visit Stoke City in a Coronation match. This season, he has made 11 first team appearances, scoring five goals. Last season he made 14 first team appearances and scored seven goals.

When Mr Steele resigned as Player-Manager of Mansfield Town to take over at Vale Park, the Vale were one of the bottom clubs of the Third Division (South). He led the team in a revival which took them to half-way in the table, and this season – his first full one with the club – he has guided the team to the runners-up position in the Third Division (North), a feat he also accomplished for Mansfield a few seasons ago.

TONIGHT'S MATCH

Though the Third Division (North) championship issue was settled yesterday evening in Oldham's Athletic's favour Port Vale, already assured of the runners-up position, can narrow the margin to one point by completing their season with a win over Grimsby Town at Vale Park this evening.

The Vale may make a forward line change from the team which won at Barrow last Saturday, for Cunliffe's name has been added to the five forwards who played last week. Grimsby, who, on their own ground, were held to a draw by the Vale, are using their end-of-the-season matches to "blood" young players. They won at Crewe last night, but for tonight's game Daley replaces Williams in goal and Dennis Smith may take over from Freeburn at right-back for his First League game.

The teams will be:-

PORT VALE:-
Hancock, Turner, Potts, Mullard, Cheadle, Sproson, Askey, Leake, Hayward, Griffiths, Hulligan, Cunliffe.

GRIMSBY TOWN:-
Daley, Freeburn, (or Smith), Robson, Grant, MacMillan, Walker, Lloyd, Lord, Smith, Johnston, Maddison.

Kick-off 6.30 p.m.
30 April 1953

Albert Leake (right) on the attack during a game against West Ham. Albert joined Vale from Stoke City in February 1950 and went on to make 291 League and Cup appearances for the Valiants.

Freddie Steele was one of Port Vale's most loved and respected managers. His management of the club led the team to their impressive 1954 FA Cup run.

Crowd scenes at Vale Park when the Valiants secured promotion to the Second Division at the end of the 1953-54 season.

Stan Turner was an integral player in the 1954 'Iron Curtain'. He made his debut for Vale in December 1950 against Northampton Town and won a Third Division (North) Championship medal in the 1953-54 season.

Vale victory and then shield presentation

By K.S.R.

The immense possibilities of the Port Vale venture were referred to when the Vale were presented with the Third Division (North) Championship Shield after their 2-0 victory over Wrexham at Vale Park last Saturday.

The shield was presented by Mr A.H. Oakley, Senior Vice-President of the Football League, who after congratulating the club, said the Vale were entering a higher and more difficult sphere, but he hoped they would advance to First Division eminence. He also praised the Vale Park Stadium.

Receiving the shield, Mr F.W. Burgess, Chairman of Port Vale, spoke of a proud day in a proud season and thanked the Manager, the team captain and the players, who were chiefly responsible for it.

Addressing the 18,300 spectators who had crowded in front of the Directors' Stand, the Manager, Mr Fred Steele said: "I hope this is the forerunner of a great future, for we want to keep marching forwards. Our success has been in the combination known as Port Vale, in which Directors, officials, players and staff have all contributed their share."

Cheers punctuated all the speeches and the biggest went to Tom Cheadle, the Vale captain, who thanked the supporters for their encouragement throughout the season.

It was fitting that the Vale should mark the day with a win and should be at full strength for the first time since their sixth round Cup-tie at Leyton. The game, however, was not a distinguished one and once Wrexham's early challenge had been subdued, the Vale should have progressed to a handsome score.

In the second half Wrexham were handicapped when left-back McGowan was taken to hospital with a fractured collar-bone. Before this, they had promised to be equal to the Vale in everything except zest in attack.

Richards and Gwatkin, the Wrexham wingers, promised well at the start but their effectiveness wilted as their inside forwards fell under the influence of the Vale's strong half-back line of Mullard, Cheadle and Sproson. Cheadle had a recurrence of this thigh injury, but was able to complete the match.

By the interval the Vale's command was increasing, but it was not until the second half that the goals came. Griffiths' headed through Askey's centre in the 55th minute and Cunliffe, following a pass from Hayward, scored the second in the 74th minute.

Griffiths had other scoring chances, Leake headed twice on to the bar and Hayward saw his header nodded from under the bar by Spruce. But while the ill-luck had a hand in keeping the score down, misguided finishing played a bigger part.

Askey was the leading light in many of the Vale's raids and Cunliffe and Hayward were also prominent in some stern duels with the Wrexham defenders. It was a hard-fought finish with Wrexham gamely battling it out against more powerful opponents.

Though the Vale should have had a bigger score, the goals which did decide the match were refreshing after the three goalless Easter games; and by again not conceding a goal, the Vale moved a step nearer to achieving a League defensive record.

20 April 1954

Chapter Two
1953-54 FA Cup run

One of Port Vale's most glorious moments in their club history and the season that made Vale a household name! Rarely has a Third Division team come so close to winning the sought after FA Cup title. Freddie Steele's hard work of the previous season was finally bearing fruit and Port Vale were an intimidating side.

The first round match against Darlington at Feethams resulted in a 3-1 win for Vale. In the second round Vale were drawn against Southport. The first match at Haig Avenue resulted in a 1-1 draw. This meant a re-play at Vale's home ground resulting in a solid 2-0 win.

Vale's confidence and surety were growing and the team were working well together. Steele had crafted a solid defence that was affectionately known as the 'Iron Curtain'.The third round match was against Queens Park Rangers where Vale secured a 1-0 win which took them safely into the fourth round to play against First Division side Cardiff City.

Thanks to goals by Albert Leake and Ken Griffiths Vale beat Cardiff City 2-0 in January 1954. The Valiants were through to the fifth round of the FA Cup and the team they were to be pitted against next were the current Cup holders Blackpool. The Blackpool team included local legend, Sir Stanley Matthews. The pace of this match can only be described as fast and furious. Vale showed an enormous amount of class and spirit that ensured a 2-0 win against the formidable First Division side.

The Valiants went through to the sixth round of the tournament and faced fellow third division side Leyton Orient. Another superb goal by Albert Leake meant Vale were through to the Semi-finals of the 1953-54 FA Cup. The team they were set to play against were First Division West Bromwich Albion.

Although a superb effort was made by Port Vale they narrowly missed achieving the coveted FA Cup title. A decision to disallow a goal by Leake due to the referee calling the goal offside meant that Vale's FA hopes quickly disappeared and ex-Vale player Ronnie Allen made the final goal for West Brom who went on to win the Cup by beating Preston in the final.

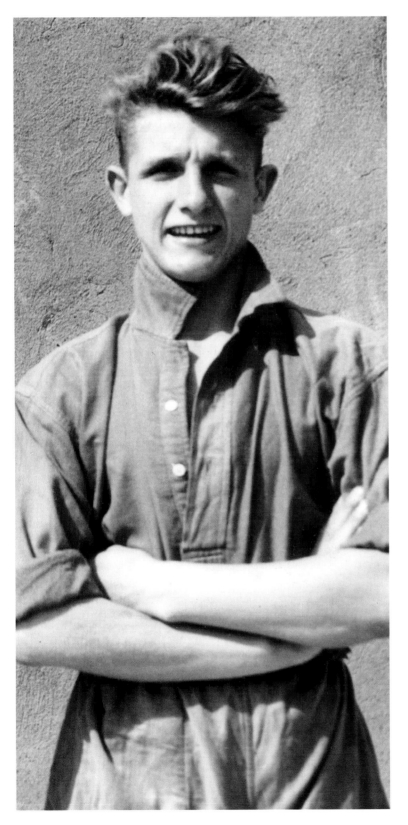

Winger Colin Askey was a crucial player in Vale's 1954 FA Cup run. His performances at that time led to many of the top clubs making inquiries into his availability. Askey remained with the club until the 1957-58 season. He went on to play for Walsall and Mansfield Town before finishing his career in non-league football.

All roads lead to Burslem!

HEAVY GOING FOR
THE BIG MATCH

TOUTS BUSY: £1 FOR 2s 6d TICKETS

Blackpool supporters were offering 2s.6d. ground tickets for as much as 15s. and £1 as early crowds swarmed on all roads to Vale Park for today's Fifth Round Cup-tie between Port Vale and Blackpool.

With the Vale ground tested for the first time to a maximum capacity of 42,000, Burslem was this morning coping with its biggest Cup-tie invasion in history.

Today's sun was a welcome sight to players and supporters alike, but it was obvious that, after yesterday's rain, the going would be heavy.

The eyes of North Staffordshire sportsmen everywhere turned to Vale Park where this afternoon

Port Vale meet Blackpool, the Cup-holders, in one of the most attractive fixtures of the day.

Possibly the first arrivals at Vale Park were two Blackpool supporters offering 2s.6d. ground tickets for £1 and 15s. At the time there was only a handful of local supporters awaiting the possibility of returned tickets.

"Too much," one of the Vale supporters commented. But nevertheless the Blackpool salesmen did business and had hopes of doing more as other people arrived.

At 10.15 Stanley Matthews strolled alone into Vale Park took a look at the ground on which groundsmen were engaged and commented, looking at the sun: "It's a pity this weather didn't arrive earlier."

For it was generally believed that yesterday's rain soaking the pitch would be more helpful to Port Vale than to the visiting team.

It was the first time in the history of the mother town that Burslem was called upon to bear the brunt of a big cup-tie

invasion and the capacity of Vale Park was being really tested for the first time by a 42,000 all-ticket gate.

For the town it was like Bank Holiday in reverse with unprecedented crowd scenes, for the seasiders had taken up their full allocation of 10,500 tickets.

This morning Blackpool had the biggest football exodus since Cup final day last year.

The Blackpool supporters arrived in seven special trains, in scores of buses, and in private cars.

THE REMAINING 31,500 TICKET HOLDERS WERE DRAWN FROM ALL THE POTTERIES TOWNS AND A WIDER AREA OF NORTH STAFFORDSHIRE AND SOUTH CHESHIRE SO THAT ALL ROADS LED TO BURSLEM.

So as to relieve town congestion as much as possible of the football, road traffic from Blackpool and the north was being diverted at Tunstall to High Lane where provision had been made for the accommodation of at least 150 buses.

In the city, arrangements had been made for 100 police to be on duty to cope with the crowds inside and outside the ground and at other control points.

Special trains were arriving between 11.32 and 1.47. There was an average of 500 passengers per train. Three brought supporters direct to Burslem station and the remainder to Longport. At both stations loudspeaker announcements guided the visitors.

After the match the first of the return trains will leave Burslem at 5 o'clock and Longport at 5.40. The last special will leave about 6.30.

20 February 1954

Vale outplay cup holders
By K.S.R

LEAKE GOALS PAVED WAY TO THE SIXTH ROUND. MATTHEWS KEPT IN CHECK.

Before a record crowd of 42,000, Port Vale shocked the star-studded Blackpool team in this afternoon's Fifth Round Cup-tie at Vale Park by a brilliant first half display in which Albert Leake put the Potteries team two goals in front. And magnificent goals they were too!

It was thrilling, forceful football with the Vale's hard-fighting, "quick-on-the-ball" play smothering Blackpool's inclination to close passing and intricate approach work. Even Matthews was kept well in check by the cast-iron Vale defence. But it was in attack as well as defence that the Vale proved more than a match for the Cupholders.

Port Vale continued in the ascendant in the second half and for every Blackpool attack generally answered with three of their own. There, were, however, one of two anxious moments for the home supporters, particularly when a ding-dong battle near the edge of the penalty area tested the solid Vale defence a quarter-of-an-hour from the finish.

The Vale Park Stadium looked an ideal setting for its greatest day since the opening on August 25th, 1950, and early spectators were surprised to find the pitch in far better condition than had been expected.

Sacks, which had been used to soak up much of the water in the middle, had been removed and the ground had been rolled and sanded. With a sunny afternoon to top the picture, the ground looked a treat for this cup battle with the going soft but not half so treacherous as it might have been after the week's rain.

Teams: -

PORT VALE: King, Turner, Potts, Mullard, Cheadle, Sproson, Askey, Leake, Hayward, Griffiths, Cunliffe.

BLACKPOOL: Farm, Shimwell, Frith, Fenton, Johnston, Kelly, Matthews, Taylor, Stephenson, Brown, Perry.

REFEREE: M H. Jackson of Leeds.

The Vale kicked off facing the sun and Hamil-road end. The Vale were the first to the penalty area with a lob from Sproson, but Blackpool quickly cleared and started a counter-attack in which Matthews took part. The visitors, however, were held just over the halfway line.

The Vale struck back with two quick raids. Following a pass from Mullard, Askey broke away along the right and Fenton, in order to check the Vale winger's centre, had to head out for a corner-kick.

Hayward leapt above a crowd of players to reach Askey's corner-kick and headed down a ball which went narrowly outside the Blackpool upright. That was a close one for Blackpool.

Later, Perry tried to break through for Blackpool on their left, but was checked by Potts and Cheadle. Later, Turner and Mullard confidently broke up another Blackpool advance down the middle.

It was a fast, exciting start with raids being exchanged at a terrific pace and there was a great cheer when Potts cut across to whip the ball off Matthews' toes a split second after the Blackpool winger had skipped round Cunliffe. Potts later put through a fine low pass for Cunliffe, but when the Vale winger tried to slip the ball inside, Fenton intervened.

Sproson sent a pass across to the unmarked Cunliffe who beat Shimwell but sent the ball straight to Fenton.

Brown opened up an attack for Blackpool with a long cross field pass to Matthews, but the winger's long swinging return went well behind Perry. In the next minute however, Matthews, playing in the middle, slipped a short pass to Taylor who set it rolling for Brown to run on and shoot over the Vale bar. It was thrilling forceful play.

A chance followed for the Vale at the other end, but Leake's shot hit a defender's leg. Askey and Leake combined to check Taylor and set themselves on an advance which ended when Askey was unable to reach a fast return pass from Hayward.

The Vale were awarded a free-kick, but Blackpool promptly took the opportunity for a raid, there was another cheer when Potts, though on the ground, again prevented Matthews from getting away with the ball.

Taking a pass from Sproson, Askey in a splendid run, started the best move so far. He sent a swift, well-judged pass out to Hayward on the right and, though Hayward's low centre was missed by the players in the goalmouth, it carried on to the unmarked Cunliffe and the Vale outside-left promptly let fly with a shot which was deflected by a defender for a corner-kick.

From this, Cunliffe sent an excellent centre for which Leake rose to head a glorious goal in the 14th minute. This was fully deserved, for in the early hard exchanges the Vale had put in more fire than Blackpool. A few minutes later Hayward forced Johnston to concede another corner-kick near the flag post. This time Cunliffe placed the ball close to the Blackpool goalmouth and Farm had to turn the ball over the bar.

Askey took this next corner-kick and, following it, Blackpool had to scramble the ball away. If the Vale forwards had been a little quicker on the draw they might well have shot through a second goal.

The Vale were fighting hard for

the ball and this was gaining them much ground and also discouraged Blackpool's inclination to close passing and intricate approach.

When Matthews and Taylor got together to try and weave a way through, first Cunliffe, then Potts and eventually Griffiths all joined in a successful covering up to stop the Blackpool pair. Later, Blackpool staged a sustained attack in the middle, but the Vale resolutely defended until they eventually cleared the ball.

So far, Cheadle and his colleagues were showing that they were not overawed by the star-studded Blackpool forward line. This strong show by the Vale rearguard encouraged the Vale for further keen challenges, and a great effort by the Vale brought them a second goal in the 26th minute.

Cunliffe placed a pass out to Hayward on the left and, from near the corner-flag, Hayward sent a low pass into the Blackpool goalmouth where Leake raced in to shoot it into the net. It was a splendid piece of work.

Blackpool then launched a fierce counter attack, but it failed when Matthews' cross-field pass carried too far. The Vale immediately replied, and both Hayward and Griffiths came near to forcing an anxious Farm to concede

further goals. After half an hour's play the Vale conceded Blackpool their first corner-kick but this was cleared, though later King had to collect a header from Stephenson.

A few minutes later, when Stephenson tried a long speculative shot a few yards outside the right hand corner of the penalty area, he forced King to a spectacular one-handed save. But this was followed by an even more brilliant save at the other end when the Vale's Cunliffe raced ahead of all opposition to force the advancing Farm to a desperate plunge in the mud.

FOLLOWING THIS, ASKEY CROSSED A DANGEROUS CENTRE. FARM MISJUDGED THE BALL AND HAYWARD, STANDING BEHIND HIM, WAS ONLY INCHES FROM REACHING IT IN FRONT OF AN OPEN GOAL.

However, there was a close shave for the Vale in the 35th minute when, following Perry's corner kick, the ball was pushed into the goalmouth near the foot of the upright where Matthews was standing. King,

however, managed to get a foot to the ball to hook it out for the Vale defence to clear. The midfield was becoming badly churned up, but Matthews – who so far was not seeing a great deal of the ball, and, when he did, was being given little chance by the close covering Vale defence to shine – was still wandering into the middle. But Blackpool were trying hard to reply to the Vale's two-goal lead, and one of their efforts saw King dive brilliantly to hold another long range drive from Stephenson.

Then came a Vale attack with Farm comfortably collecting a long ground shot from Hayward. But Blackpool broke away again and this time for Matthews to show something of the skill for which he is so much famed. He worked the ball almost to the touchline, and then brought it along, passing Sproson on his way to send a low short pass into the goalmouth. Taylor tried a quick shot, only to see King save once again.

Though upchurned mud had a spoiling effect on much of the midfield play, the Vale were exploiting the firmer wing areas to much more advantage than Blackpool had so far done. The Vale packed their defence in determination whenever Blackpool threatened but most of the threat had so far come from the Vale who, with a dashing and thrustful leader in Hayward, had set a cracking pace with keen tackling and first time passing and shooting.

The Blackpool defenders, despite Johnston's coolness in the middle, had been clearly worried and the Vale were well worth their 2-0 advantage at this stage on an inspired showing. Blackpool had in Stephenson a leader who showed he had a powerful shot when given the chance and in this half he had been Blackpool's most dangerous forward, even though Cheadle was keeping a very close watch on him.

HALF-TIME:-
PORT VALE 2
BLACKPOOL 0

The play resumed much in the same tempo with the eager Vale forwards attacking alternatively on the left and then the right. The Vale were obviously not going to rest on the laurels gained in the first half, but were striving for further goals which looked likely as Cunliffe and Askey crossed some dangerous centres.

Blackpool eventually broke away, only for Turner to check Perry. Then a long pass found Askey, the Vale outside-right,

who sent a low pass into the middle to Griffiths who raced ahead of Johnston and shot past Farm who was running out. But the shot hit the foot of Blackpool's upright and rebounded into play. That was another close escape for Blackpool and it was soon followed by another near miss when Hayward's header was only inches wide.

Once again Blackpool struck back but King saved Fenton's drive. The Vale replied with a smart raid along the right between Askey and Hayward, but Hayward's centre was caught by Farm. This was the same thrilling pace as the first half and this was a match packed with incident as a cup-tie should be.

Blackpool were awarded a free-kick on the edge of the Vale penalty area, but Brown's drive hit Cheadle on the body and flew for a corner-kick. The corner was cleared and the Vale built up a raid which led to Hayward dashing after a ball and colliding with Farm.

The Blackpool goalkeeper was treated on the field for what was apparently an injury to his knee, but he was able to carry on. What Blackpool raids there had been in this half so far had been down the middle or on their left flank and, against these, Cheadle, Turner and Mullard had put up a commanding fight.

Matthews was a lone figure on the right and once again the ball was rarely going through to him.

On the other hand the Vale's outside-right Askey was seeing plenty of action and was making a useful contribution to the Vale's effort. Turner smartly checked Brown's progress, but at a later attempt Brown managed to swing across a pass which eventually reached Matthews. The winger, however, sliced his centre and it swerved to Sproson who promptly swept the ball up-field for Cunliffe to set the Vale on the move again. These efforts eventually led to a dangerous centre from Askey which Farm punched with one hand out for a corner, but injured himself in the process.

Cunliffe took the corner-kick and when Farm dropped the ball in his goalmouth the Blackpool defenders had a hectic scramble before they got it away. This was a dour fight all the way with every yard being contested and with the Vale still the more dangerous side.

In blocking a fierce drive from Griffiths just inside the penalty area, Kelly was hurt and had to receive attention. Later, King went down to stop a drive from Taylor. At this point, Blackpool were fighting hard but though

Prelude to a big cup-tie shock. Vale's captain Tom Cheadle shakes hands with Harry Johnston, captain of FA Cup holders Blackpool before the kick-off in the fifth round David and Goliath contest at Vale Park in February 1954. Vale won this contest 2-0.

Matthews got possession and slipped a pass across, a resourceful Vale defence once more quickly sealed up the gap.

But for every Blackpool attack the Vale generally answered with about three, and Mullard and Sproson gave great service, both in supporting these attacks and in meeting Blackpool's counter offensive. Sproson, after cunningly beating two Blackpool defenders slipped a pass out to Cunliffe and from the outside-left's centre Hayward went very close to scoring with a header.

So far this had not been Matthews' day and this was probably due in the main to the conditions. The fact that the Blackpool efforts to adapt themselves did not include a prominent role for him,

and also to the Vale's quick tackling and covering up. Towards the close Blackpool gained one of their rare corner-kicks and in helping to clear following the centre, Mullard injured his right knee. After attention he resumed limping, but the Vale kept fighting and when Hayward tripped with Johnston in the Blackpool penalty area there were appeals for a penalty kick, but the referee waved play on.

It was a finish which saw the Vale still the stronger, fitter side and still pressing, but it also saw Mullard on the running track receiving further attention from the Vale's trainer Ken Fish. Mullard was limping with a blanket round his shoulders.

20 February 1954

Vale's opening goal against Blackpool was a blistering shot from Albert Leake which goalkeeper George Farm and defenders Frith and Shimwell failed to stop. Even the Wizard of Dribble, Stanley Matthews, couldn't save Blackpool from a shock 2-0 defeat after being kept well in check by the cast-iron Vale defence.

Flamboyant Blackpool fans entertain the 42,000 strong crowd at Vale Park before the fifth-round FA Cup match. Blackpool were odds-on favourites to go through to the sixth round.

Port Vale in cup semi-final
by K.S.R

LEYTON ORIENT:
Groombridge, Evans, Charlton, Blizzard, Aldous, Mallett, Facey, Pacey, Rees, Morgan, Poulton.

PORT VALE:
King, Turner, Potts, Mullard, Cheadle, Sproson, Askey, Leake, Hayward, Griffiths, Cunliffe.

WORTHY WINNERS
OF STORMING
GAME AT LEYTON.

LEAKE AGAIN
SCORES THE
DECIDING GOAL.

Port Vale are in the Semi-Final of the F.A. Cup competition!

They made football history this afternoon when, by defeating Leyton Orient in the sixth round tie on the London club's ground, they became only the second Third Division club ever to reach the semi-final. Nearly 8,000 North Staffordshire supporters cheered the team on to victory and there were scenes of tremendous enthusiasm when the final whistle sounded and the Vale's followers mobbed the players.

In a rousing game – fast, vigorous and exciting – Leake, who scored the all-important goals against Blackpool in the last round, did it again after 19 minutes of this all-action game. The Orient fought back to give the Vale defenders a testing time.

They stood firm against a terrific challenge and in the closing minutes King, in goal, distinguished himself with a truly magnificent save. It was thrills all the way – to the last kick of a match, truly memorable for North Staffordshire.

The weather was dull but dry when the Port Vale team arrived at the Brisbane-road ground, where they found the small compact pitch in a firm condition, but uneven and with hardly any grass except in the corner areas.

The Vale were unchanged for their ninth successive match – which meant they had the same team that had accounted for Darlington, Southport, Queen's Park Rangers, Cardiff and Blackpool in the preceding rounds.

Orient welcomed back their Welsh International leader, Rees, and were also at full strength.

The game opened at a cracking pace with tackles and passes having a touch of desperation right from the start. Lively work by the forwards brought both defences into fighting action. But when the first real threat developed from Morgan's pass to Rees on the Orient right flank, Sproson stepped neatly in to take the ball and clear.

A Vale raid followed but back came Orient. Following a centre from Poulton, it twice needed Cheadle's head to nod the ball away from the Vale goalmouth and prevent Orient getting in a shot. Turner also put some good work for the Vale against this early Orient pressure, but later Morgan shot over the bar and a few minutes later King comfortably collected a tame header from Pacey.

It was a sticky, bouncing ball the players had to deal with and most of them – on both sides – were inclined to keep it moving by hitting it first-time and taking the risk whether their passes carried any accuracy or not. This gave much of the play a hurried and open look.

King held Poulton's centre from a corner-kick and then the Vale retaliated with smart raids along both wings, but could not wrest a shooting position from the barrier laid down by the sharp-tackling Orient defenders. Aldous and Blizzard were prominent in another Leyton offensive which was beaten off.

After a period of strongly contested exchanges the Vale struck hard to take the lead in the 19th minute. Askey's centre from a corner-kick was headed down by Hayward and Leake – who scored the two goals which defeated Blackpool in the last round – promptly flashed a low drive past Groombridge into the far corner of the net. The goal was greeted with wild enthusiasm by the large North Staffordshire contingent.

A few minutes later Hayward broke clean through but his shot was pulled down by Groombridge.

Hayward was a most energetic leader of the Vale line and several times showed Aldous how dangerous he could be if given the slightest chance. Griffiths gave useful assistance at this stage and Cunliffe and

Askey were lively on the wings. But Orient were obviously not disheartened by their set-back and in no time launched a sustained counter offensive to force several corner-kicks. With Sproson and Mullard working in close unison with Cheadle and his full-backs, the Vale defended magnificently.

Orient were held and then pushed back into their own half. In the 30th minute the Vale might have gone further ahead when Hayward and Griffiths diverted an Askey corner-kick along to Cunliffe who, from close range, sent a fierce drive over the bar.

Orient quickly hit back and during a scramble in the Vale goalmouth Poulton, their outside-left, was injured and had to be carried off the field on a stretcher. Port Vale, having resisted the early Orient pressure, were now looking the surer in defensive strategy in what was proving a real Cup-tie thriller, with plenty of incident and exciting play. As the more methodical approach work also came from the Vale at this point, they had a definite advantage.

Two chances to go further ahead were narrowly missed by the Vale – first when Griffiths, taking a pass from Hayward, skimmed the bar with his shot and a few minutes later when inter-passing between Askey and Leake led to Cunliffe

heading on to the roof of the Orient net from Askey's centre.

Orient, nevertheless, were still fighting hard and forced yet another corner-kick. But as fast as they put in a raid so did the Vale retaliate with moves carrying greater threat and persistence. Leake tested Groombridge with a long drive and then Cunliffe put the ball over the bar.

In the closing minutes of this half Orient caught the Vale "on the wrong foot" but King gallantly dived at Rees' feet and then, after a further collision, scrambled up yet again to push the ball away over Morgan's head. In this daring piece of work – for which he earned ovation from the crowd – King injured his side and had to receive attention. The Vale had justified their narrow advantage.

HALF-TIME:- LEYTON ORIENT 0 PORT VALE 1

Poulton was able to resume his original position when the teams came out for the second half, having had a stitch put in a cut over his left eye. King was also on duty. But another piece of drama came within two minutes of the restart.

Hayward escaped up the right and sent over a beautiful low centre, which appeared to give Griffiths an excellent chance. However, Groombridge rushed out to dive at the Vale inside-left's feet and both players went down, the ball rolling clear. Both were hurt, but both were able to carry on after the trainer's attention.

And then, at the other end, Cheadle slipped and gave Rees the opportunity for a long shot which went wide. Cunliffe built up a Vale raid but his pass along the ground was intercepted before it could reach Hayward. Eventually, the ball went loose to Mullard who, with a splendid low drive, brought Groombridge to a save at the foot of the upright.

It was now raining slightly but there was the same pace and vigour about the play as in the first half. Raid was exchanged for raid and with only one goal separating the teams, it was still "anybody's game" – even though the Vale had been the more aggressive.

Cheadle, Potts and Turner fought stubbornly and showed wonderful resource in curbing the Orient's forwards in this hurly-burly of a tie. It was a fight all the way, with every player having a severe test in stamina in all-out effort during gruelling challenge and counter-challenge.

Sproson, with a long dropping shot, forced Groombridge to gather the ball under the bar and later Groombridge pulled down with one hand a Cunliffe header.

There was frequent promise of goals, despite great defensive work. Rees headed over the Vale bar, and shortly afterwards a tense spell of several seconds followed in the Vale goalmouth before the defence got the ball properly cleared. Though this was by no means a classic game – with the football the Vale served up at Cardiff and against Blackpool unsuited to this occasion – it was tough and thrilling and of more typical Cup-tie character. There were great honours at stake and these were being terrifically contested.

Orient's inside men showed little inclination to shoot and Charlton, the home left-back, tried to show them the way by racing through and letting fly from long range. The ball flashed just a yard outside the post. Orient missed an opportunity when Facey sent over a perfectly placed lob but Rees, in front of goal, made contact with the top of his head instead of his forehead and the ball went well over.

Up to the very last minute Orient kept up strenuous efforts to force a replay and the end of this stiffly fought tie was as

thrilling as it had been all the way from the start. Just before the end Poulton cut through from the left and with a clever rising drive brought King brilliantly to turn the ball over the bar.

Almost immediately afterwards, at the other end, Hayward, taking a pass from Askey, moved in from the right and had Groombridge diving to push the ball away. With only a few seconds to go Orient were awarded a corner-kick and excitement reached fever pitch as a struggle took place in the Vale goalmouth until an Orient player headed the ball over the bar.

But, despite this closely fought game, this was the Vale's day – and once again it was their brilliant teamwork and ability to adapt themselves to the opposition and conditions which deservedly gave them the victory. There were great scenes of enthusiasm from the Vale supporters who rushed across the pitch to congratulate the players.

13 March 1954

MATCH INCIDENTS AS SEEN FROM THE TOUCHLINE

Basil Hayward, the Vale centre-forward, jumps with a challenge to Orient's flying goalkeeper Groombridge, but the ball sails far out of reach

One of the most thrilling moments in the game. Goalkeeper King making a truly magnificent save on the goalline from Poulton's scorching shot—the incident which really marked the end of Orient's bid to rescue the game.

Here is another Vale challenge, with Groombridge punching clear from the leaping Hayward, who led the Vale line with skill and dash.

Orient left-winger Poulton was injured—a head cut, needing stitches—when King here beat him to the ball. In the foreground is Turner, the Vale right-back.

Injury, too, was the outcome of this spectacular incident. Groombridge dives to the feet of the Vale inside-left, Griffiths. He received a knock on the knee and was consequently unable to play in a League game earlier this week.

With the Vale under intense pressure, Cheadle and Sproson hold up the Orient forwards, Mullard being handy in case of need and King on the alert. The referee, on the spot, keeps a keen eye on the play.

Two pictorial supplements
featured in the Sentinel
during the 1954 FA Cup run.

The goal that took Port Vale into the FA Cup Semi-final against West Bromwich Albion at Villa Park.
Orient keeper Groombridge and Vale's Ken Griffiths watch the ball cross the line while Albert Leake
throws up his arms as he realises that he has scored.

Leyton Orient under attack in the FA Cup Tie, 13 March 1954.

Alcocks

RALEIGH
RUDGE
HUMBER
ROBIN HOOD
Cash or Terms

Market Place ... BURSLEM Phone 81575
15 High St. ... HANLEY (still waiting)
50 High St. ... TUNSTALL Phone 84500

Staffordshire
Weekly Sentinel
COUNTY, AGRICULTURAL, AND PICTORIAL NEWSPAPER

POTTERIES
EDITION

FOR INDIGESTION AND ALL
KINDRED AILMENTS TAKE
BOOTS
Essence of Life Pills

No. 5,214.—Est. 1854.   Registered at the General Post Office.   **FRIDAY, FEBRUARY 19, 1954**   Telephone: Stoke-on-Trent 3281   P   N   TWOPENCE

PORT VALE FOOTBALLERS PREPARE FOR THEIR BIG TEST

Port Vale's F.A. Cup tie with Blackpool has caught the imagination of the sporting public not only in this district but in all parts of the country, and a "full house" of 42,000 is assured to-morrow. Here the goalkeeper, Ray King, who has been beaten fewer times than any other league keeper, shows his agility, and the captain, Tom Cheadle, gets in some heading practice.

Caught by the camera in the corner of the net, five of the Vale players typify the team's happy spirit.

Ball practice, and more ball practice, is said to be the keynote of success, and Cunliffe, Sproson and Potts, Turner, Mullard, and Askey, Hayward and Griffiths are seen using heads and feet.

After the field training the Port Vale players enjoy a bath and trim-up in one of the most luxurious dressing rooms in the country.

While King and Cunliffe finish dressing, Griffiths and Turner scan the papers, which have featured the match as one of the most attractive games of the day. Then, training over, members of the team relax with their Manager, Mr. Fred Steele.

This incredible picture was featured on the front page of the Evening Sentinel on Saturday, March 20 1954. It shows crowds of 40,000 strong queuing at Vale Park in the hopes of securing a ticket for the all-important Vale and West Bromwich Semi-final FA Cup match. The ticket offices opened at 1 o'clock and by 2.30pm ticket allocations were exhausted. Many fans had to be turned away in bitter disappointment.

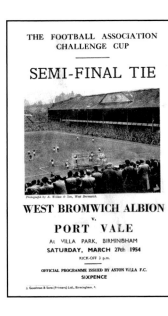

The front cover of the programme from Port Vale's famous match against West Bromwich Albion in 1954. The 'official' programme was only 6d at the time.

After an incredible cup-run the Valiants finally competed against West Bromwich Albion in the 1954 FA Cup Semi-final. Vale seized the lead after 40 minutes of play when Albert Leake scored the first goal. Albion equalised in the second half and former Vale player Ronnie Allen took them into the lead with their second goal of the match. Leake made another attempt to equalise but his goal was disallowed as the referee ruled that they were offside. This decision saw the Valiants FA Cup hopes diasappear.

Ray King is beaten at Villa Park in 1954, when Vale lost to West Bromwich Albion 2-1.

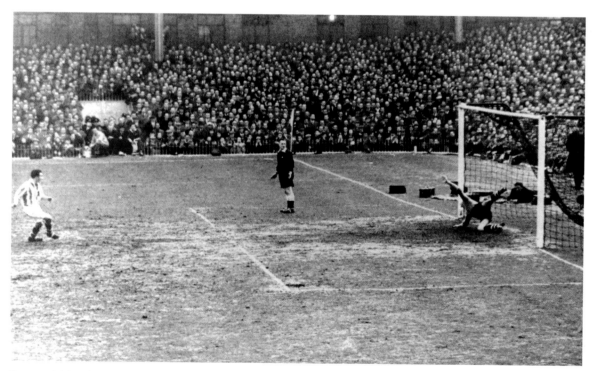

Former Vale player Ronnie Allen, scores the decisive penalty for West Brom and destroys the Valiants 1954 FA Cup hopes.

Ronnie Allen takes a shot against Ray King in the FA Cup Semi-final match between Vale and West Bromwich Albion. Sproson and Potts watch on as the ball goes wide.

Roy Sproson recalls his 828 Games - and that '54 Cup Semi-final.

JUST ONE STEP
FROM WEMBLEY –
THEN A DISPUTED
PENALTY
KNOCKED US OUT.

Having played 800 and more games for Port Vale, time has dulled my memory of the majority, but there are a handful that I can recall as if they were yesterday.

My debut is not among them, other than the fact I was naturally nervous and that it was a fine day. I do not recall much of that appearance against Gillingham back in November 1950.

What is clearer is my home debut at Vale Park against Bournemouth. We won 3-1 and I missed a great scoring chance from a matter of yards. Also,

every throw I took seemed to be a foul and I sustained an injury that kept me out for about five weeks.

Then there was my first League goal, scored against Torquay, in a 1-1 draw. Alan Bennett crossed the ball from the left and I found the inside of the near post with a header. That was at the Hamil end.

GAME IN A GALE

Another goal I recall in the early days was against Oldham in the 1952-53 season. They became champions of the Third Division (North) that term and finished runners-up. We won at Oldham and were held to a 1-1 draw at Vale.

I have played in all manner of weather and will never forget a game at Scunthorpe, which was played in a gale. The wind was so strong that it carried off the roof of the stand and it once took me three minutes to take a throw in. Every time I parted

with the ball it kept going out of play. We had many stirring F.A.Cup encounters, especially those on the way to the semi-finals in 1954. I remember going to Cardiff, then of the First Division, for a match that was doubtful because of the conditions.

All the lads were nervous and conflicting reports reached us while we were in the snooker room of the hotel on the morning of the game.

We sighed with relief when told the match was off, then fear returned when it was on. The pitch, hard and icy, was eventually declared fit and we won 2-0 in a tremendous battle.

I will always remember the duel between Tommy Cheadle and Cardiff's Trevor Ford. Pound for pound they were probably the two hardest men I have known, yet they came off with a smile and handshake at the finish, battered and bruised having gone at each other hammer and tongs for 90 minutes!

Then there was the reception afterwards when we reached Cardiff station. It was a sea of Vale faces. An incredible sight.

In the sixth round we travelled to Orient – or Leyton Orient in those days – and this was a terrible game to play in.

Both teams were nervous and, on a bumpy pitch the ball was never still. It was whacked from end to end and one goal to us was enough to settle it.

INJURY FEAR

The realisation that we, a Third Division side, were in the semi-finals frightened us a little. Nobody really wanted to play before the big match for fear of being injured but we did not worry about who we would meet, be it Preston, West Bromwich or Sheffield Wednesday.

At the time, we did not know what it was like to lose and the thought never occurred to us. We were convinced, in fact, that we could not be beaten.

The build-up to the game against West Bromwich at Villa Park was wonderful. Pressmen who previously had not probably even heard of Port Vale trained with us and camped on the doorstep. We had good luck letters from all over the world and the usual pleas for tickets.

When I read nowadays of players supposedly making fortunes out of selling tickets it makes me laugh because I must be the only player on record to ever to lose money from an F.A.Cup semi final. It happened like this.

In addition to my two complimentaries, I bought a couple of 2s 6d tickets for friends. One of them failed to turn up so I lost the cash and still have the tickets at home to prove it.

Furthermore, despite all the money the club must have made that day, we received nothing more than our basic wage.

We stayed overnight in an hotel in Droitwich and although we were naturally nervous, we were not as concerned as we were before the Leyton Orient tie.

We were a big, strong, physical side and quickly settled down against Albion who, I believe, were top of the First Division at the time. We were a goal up early on and by half time we seriously thought the game was as good as over.

West Bromwich gave us no problems at all and it was a poor goal to concede which gave them an equaliser. Tommy Cheadle headed the ball away and it was lobbed back into the net.

What really made us mad was the goal shortly afterwards which we had disallowed.

Colin Askey beat two men in a great run to the byeline before pulling the ball back for Albert Leake to crack home, and we protested strongly when the referee ruled Colin offside.

BITTER MOMENT

It was a bitter moment and then came the controversial penalty, which cost us the game. The incident happened behind me so I could not see it but on viewing a clip of film afterwards it looked as though Lee had taken a good three steps before falling in the box. Ronnie Allen, a former Vale player, of course, banged the spot kick into the net and we were out.

The Vale team went to Wembley to see the final between West Bromwich and Preston and we were convinced that we were better than both finalists.

It was that disallowed goal that upset us more than the penalty. We felt it had been deemed that a Third Division club would not play at Wembley, almost as if it had been pre-conceived by the F.A.

Personally, I did not feel too bad about it. I quickly forgot about the game and the fact that we were Third Division champions was some consolation. We had gained promotion by Easter and clinched the championship well before the end of that remarkable season.

24 February 1975

Tom Cheadle at home with his wife and son. This picture was taken as part of the Sentinel's souvenir supplement for the FA Cup Semi-final against West Brom. They are glancing through the Weekly Sentinel pictorial record of the Valiants' 1954 Cup progress.

A portrait of family life from one of Vale's most respected captains, Tom Cheadle. His career at the club spanned nine years he is pictured here relaxing at home with his son, Peter.

Stan Turner made his debut for Port Vale in 1950 in a 1-1 draw at Northampton Town. As a strong defender he won a medal in the 1953-54 Third Division championship.

Most Glorious Period in Vale's History

By Roy Sproson

Port Vale Football Club celebrate their Centenary next year (1976) and it has been my privilege to share in the most memorable campaign in the club's history.

I refer to the 1953-54 season. We won the Third Division (North) championship by a mile and reached the semi-finals of the FA Cup.

The club must have made a mint, but the players made virtually nothing.

In fact, we had to battle to have our basic wage raised from £12-a-week to £14; this was supplemented by a £2 win bonus, which, fortunately, occurred often.

In retrospect, I wish we had an older, more experienced player among our ranks at the time; someone, for example, who had played in the First Division and knew more of what the game was about.

LOCAL BOYS

Unfortunately for us, we were all rather green. The majority of us were local boys and we had nobody to guide us when it came to cash. Sadly, it left a bitter taste with some of the players at the end of a great season.

In the league we lost three of our 46 games and conceded only 21 goals. Our "iron curtain" defence, as it became known, let in just five of those goals at Vale Park and two of them came in one game, against Chesterfield.

Our team was much the same as it had been the previous season when we finished one point behind the champions, Oldham. Freddie Steele, however, finished playing to concentrate on managing.

Having come so close the season before, there was little doubt in our minds that we would win the title in 1953-54. We thought, in fact, that it would be a formality.

A couple of positional changes took place. Basil Hayward was switched from defence to centre-forward and Albert Mullard and Albert Leake changes places, with Mullard going from inside-right to right-half and Leake vice-versa.

Ray King became our regular goalkeeper, even winning an England "B" cap, but it could so easily have been Ray Hancock, brother of Ken.

Hancock was in line as first choice but in the pre-season match between the Probables and the Possibles he was switched to the reserve team. I do not know whether he had a row with Freddie Steele, but his nose was pushed out and the first team drilled seven goals past him in that practice match.

Our first game was at Mansfield and I scored in a 2-1 win; shortly afterwards we travelled to Barrow and figured in a goalless draw.

PARALYSED

Barrow had a Scottish international playing for them who lived in Preston and he travelled with us on the train. Sitting in our compartment, he told us he was going to have £25 on us to win the championship ... and the season had hardly begun! He was a good judge. We never entertained the idea of defeat and most teams, even those from the higher divisions that we met in the Cup, were paralysed with fear at the prospect of playing us.

We were a big physical team with a good number of six-footers in the line-up and the tactics employed made scoring difficult against us.

We were termed "defensive" even in those days because we probably pioneered the 4-4-2 and 4-2-4 systems. Our wingers Colin Askey and Dickie Cunliffe, used to play deep when required, which left Hayward and Leake as the front players.

I used to think that Freddie Steele was 20 years ahead of his time when it came to tactics and another of his ploys was to deliberately get us all so keyed up to play that we could not wait to get on to the field.

He used to hold us back in the dressing room while the opposition was out kicking in so that we were like greyhounds in a trap.

I recall the cup-tie against Blackpool. The referee almost broke the door down to get us out but Fred would have none of it. We did not take to the field until the referee was in the centre circle, so there was no time for a kick about. When the whistle went we tore into them.

There were superstitions in the team, too, Freddie used to wear a tweed trilby, a pair of black and white hooped football stockings with his suit and let his hair grow long.

On the one trip north we went to see "Mother Goose" on a Friday night and had a good result the next day. Thereafter, when we were away, we used to try and find a showing of "Mother Goose." We must have seen it four times but we always won!

We also used to frequent music halls and the 14 or 15 of us would double the audience sometimes. We used to love taking the mickey out the artists and in Mr Diffin we had a Director who was something of a card himself.

He once went on stage to supposedly assist a conjurer but ended doing the tricks himself.

Team spirit was therefore tremendous, although socially the lads did not have the same harmony. We had a number of loners, like King and Tommy Cheadle; perhaps some of them did not like each other as people but on the park it was different.

I remember one game at Bradford Park Avenue. Reg Potts — who acquired the nickname "Dan" after Desperate Dan in the boys' comics — had a terribly swollen

ankle, which was all the colour of the rainbow.

No way did it seem that he could play but it was coming up to FA Cup time and the manager told him that if he did not turn out then he would lose his place.

So Reg struggled to get his boot on and turned out. The rest of the lads rallied round to cover him and although we only had 10 men, with Reg being a passenger, we won 2-0.

Our success in the league — we were often clapped on and booed off — rubbed off in the cup run.

We did, however, have an awkward match in the second round at Southport where we were outplayed for much of the time. Askey and Leake were limping for three quarters of the game yet we managed a 1-1 draw.

We did not play particularly well in the replay, either, but won 2-0 and we were on our way to those other ties with Q.P.R., Cardiff, Blackpool, Leyton Orient and finally West Bromwich Albion at Villa Park.

BROKE WRIST

We were fit and trained hard under Ken Fish, who still says that the Vale lads were the best he has ever worked with.

Goalkeeper Ray King was a quietly spoken man from the North East who used to strap his wrists before each game. He was particularly good in the air and told us that he once broke his wrist saving a penalty from Tommy Lawton.

Full-backs Reg Potts and Stan Turner were built like brick toilets and were capable, and often did, of frightening wingers to death with their aggression.

Tommy Cheadle was another quiet man on the field, but was hard as rock and the fastest mover on the books.

Albert Mullard was a good all round player and they did not come much braver that Colin Askey, who would have been the best right-winger in England with a shade more pace.

Albert Leake formed a partnership with Basil Hayward. He was a good professional, big and powerful and a good target man. Basil was supremely fit, hard and possessed a great left foot. He was strong in the air and claimed that nobody could hurt him.

Ken Griffiths had two good feet and was a lethal finisher. He could dwell on the ball, too, but was sadly vastly underrated by the crowd at Vale Park. Ken was a professional's pro, much appreciated by his fellow players.

Dickie Cunliffe was fast and direct on the left-wing and a good worker while Derek Tompkinson, almost the permanent 12th man, was more than useful to have around. I think he scored a hat-trick in one game against York and was dropped the following week when Leake was fit.

A grand bunch of players, therefore, and notably nearly all local-born players with pride in their hearts to play for Port Vale. That, sadly, is a far cry from some of the attitudes adopted today.

10 March 1975

Posing for the Sentinel's camera, as part of a special FA Cup semi-final souvenir, is Vale's right-half, Albert Mullard (right). Outside of playing football Albert was a motoring enthusiast. Standing with him is Jim Elsby, a first reserve for Vale's 1954 first team.

Ray Hancock narrowly missed out to Ray King as Vale's principal goalkeeper during the 1954 FA Cup run.

Chapter Three
1954-1959

After the fantastic FA Cup run Port Vale returned to playing solely their remaining league fixtures. The season was by no means over and they still had to work towards gaining promotion. They had to fit 12 matches into the rest of the season and it resulted in some amazing football. With tremendous wins of 7-0 against Stockport County the rest of the 1953-54 season made exciting viewing. Vale finished the season at the top of the Third Division (North) a clear 11 points in front of Barnsley. Freddie Steele's winning team had secured Port Vale promotion into the Second Division.

Port Vale never managed to repeat the FA Cup run of 1953-54 but they did secure their place in the Second Division. The club decided to expand their grounds with the addition of the new 4,500 seater Railway stand and paddock for 12,000. Their run of good fortune unfortunately did not last.

January 1957 saw the resignation of manager Freddie Steele. Vale were slipping further and further to the bottom of the Second Division and eventually by the culmination of the 1956-57 season they were relegated back to the Third Division (South). It was also a season that saw the departure of Vale's much loved captain, Tom Cheadle.

Norman Low took over from Freddie Steele as manager and instigated a new radical form of play. Gone were the days of Steele's defensive Iron Curtain and in came Low's more aggressive attack policy.

At the end of the 1957-58 season the Football League's Third Divisions North and South were reorganised into a Third and Fourth Division. Vale had finished 15th at the end of the season and so were placed into the Fourth Division.

By the end of 1958-59 Vale had worked their way to the top of the new Fourth Division and secured their promotion into the Third Division.

By the end of the fifties Vale had seen the heights and depths of the Football League. The club had undergone some significant alterations – they had moved grounds, reached the semi-final of the FA Cup, had four managers and seen some incredible players come and go from the club.

Albert Leake with his wife at home. This photograph was taken by a Sentinel photographer for the 1954 FA Cup Souvenir edition.

Steele's two against Vale

Past recalled testimonial – Not since December 6th 1952, have Port Vale been 'beaten' at home, but that happened last night (writes K.S.R.) and the man responsible Mr. Fred Steele, the Port Vale Manager!

Steele was centre-forward for an All-Star XI, who opposed a Vale team, which included eight of the Cup semi-final line-up, in a testimonial match. The All-Stars team was comprised of former players several of them past internationals who are now prominent in the administrative side of the game.

A rainy dull evening probably prevented a larger attendance. However, the entertainment value was rewarding enough, for in a sportingly contested game was served a pleasant mixture of pretty ideas, glimpses of past brilliance on one hand a rising talent on the other, light humour and youthful exuberance, and a proper dash of seriousness to make it all worthwhile.

After Barber had given the Vale side the lead, Steele quickly changed the issue to the favour of the "Stars" and became the first player to beat King twice in a match this season.

In these two incidents Steele delighted the crowd with touches of the craft that in the early part of last season served the Vale in the League. It must have seemed a long 90 minutes for most of the veteran opposition, but the gentle mode of the challenging allowed them to recall the tricks, delicacies and guile of their day and they more than made a game of it- they won.

CULTURED TOUCHES

Sammy Crooks, now Manager of Shrewsbury Town, stepped in with pace that surprised the oldest member of his side and his inside partner Raich Carter (Manager of Leeds United) supplied the tailored passes that led to the goals and shooting that very nearly recorded some for himself.

Tim Ward (Manager of Barnsley) made a lively start as inside partner to Peter Doherty (Manager of Doncaster Rovers), who later took on a roaming role, and both nearly increased their side's lead in a sudden spurt during the closing minutes. Doherty hit an upright with a rasping drive and when Carter pulled back a Steele pass Ward forced King to a flying save.

A prominent and clever wing-half display came from Joe Mercer, of Arsenal, and his colleague at right half, Bill Corkhill (Manager of Scunthorpe United) also contributed to the constructive flow to test the younger Vale players.

Les McDowell (Manager of Manchester City), as pivot, and Bert Sproston (Bolton Wanderers' trainer) and Andy Beattie (Manager of Huddersfield Town), the full-backs, made the Vale forwards work for their chances, and Frank Swift (ex-Manchester City goalkeeper) supported them with some spectacular saves.

The "old maters" did well with their cultured strokes, for the Vale gave them a lively performance. Emphasising his all-round ability was Vale's left-half Sproson, who featured in some splendid inter-passing with Leake. Cunliffe, too, showed to advantage with his speed and centres.

Port Vale went ahead after 20 minutes when Barber standing in the goalmouth, headed over the falling Swift a cross from Hulligan. Six minutes later came the equaliser from the first of Steele's goals. Receiving a long pass down the middle, Steele switched the ball out to Carter on his left, and then ran forward to hook Carter's return pass just inside the upright out of King's reach. Six minutes before the interval, Steele, accepting a long through pass again from Carter, closed in before shooting his second goal past King. Just before this, Carter and Ward had neatly manoeuvred the ball through, and Carter, with a fine drive, brought King to a skilful save.

SWIFT'S SAVES

After Swift had caught a close range shot from Cunliffe, Carter sent a long drive sweeping over the Hamil road goal and then Tomkinson did similar at the other end. Several minutes passed before there were any further shooting incidents, but two within as many minutes saw Swift collect under the bar a long lob from Cunliffe and the punch away Leake's drive.

The "stars" gamely fought against the Vale and fading stamina in the second-half, but they not only denied their opponents an equalising goal but several times went close to increasing their lead. The final whistle came just as Steele was about to take a shot following a corner-kick and so cut short what might have been a hat-trick!

Attendance 11,500

30 March 1954

Floodlit Match

Tomorrow is the day Port Vale have been waiting for since March 1954: a visit from West Bromwich Albion, the team who beat them in the FA Cup semi-final.

The occasion, however, is more of a social one than an opportunity for revenge, West Bromwich having agreed to be the first club to play under the Vale's new floodlights. West Bromwich are bringing their strongest available side. One absentee is wing-half Setters, who is playing for the England under 23 side against Poland at Hillsborough. Barlow, the skipper, is moved to wing-half and Hughes, a young Welshman, comes in at centre-half. There is a doubt about outside-left Campbell. He is to have a final fitness test tomorrow, but there is every chance that he will play.

UNCHANGED?

Barring injuries at Southport tonight, the Vale will field an unchanged team, though it is possible that Manager Low will make some alterations at half-time. The team's playing records so far this season are amazingly similar. Both are unbeaten away and both have yet to win a home game! The Vale, of course, have to avoid defeat at Southport tonight to keep their away record intact.

The opening ceremony tomorrow at 7 p.m. will be followed by a demonstration of ball control by David Burnside, the West Bromwich player. At half-time 40 hostesses from holiday camps will give an exhibition of formation marching. The Vale club have decided to publish a special souvenir programme, which will be sold outside the ground tomorrow.

The probable teams are:-

PORT VALE:
Jones, Donaldson, Martin, Whalley, Leake, Miles, Hall, Poole (H), Wilkinson, Steele, Cunliffe.

WEST BROMWICH ALBION:
Jackman, Howe, Williams, Dudley, Hughes, Barlow, Campbell, Kevan, Allen, Burnside, Hogg.

Port Vale today issued a statement denying reports that they wanted offers for certain of their players. Mr Norman Low, the Vale Manager, said:

"It is quite untrue that we are prepared to accept offers for Kinsey and Sproson and it is equally untrue that we have made offers for Bowyer, of Stoke City, or, for that matter, any one."

23 October 1958

League match Potteries fans have waited 22 years to see –
Defences Hold Fast In Stern Stoke-Vale Encounter

City Lose 100 Per Cent Record by N.G.

STOKE CITY 0
PORT VALE 0

Before a capacity crowd at the Victoria Ground this afternoon, Stoke City met Port Vale in their first League encounter for 22 years. It was a sternly fought goalless draw which robbed the City of their 100 per cent record.

Stoke were the more dangerous side in the early stages and their thrusts

sometimes had the Vale defenders kicking with more haste than accuracy. Port Vale improved, however, and the City goal was put under heavy pressure for a time, Robertson making some fine saves. Up to the interval, however, the defences – not without a struggle – managed to keep on top.

Play in the second half followed a similar pattern with Stoke City first doing most of the attacking against a well packed Vale defence and the Vale making their effort in the last quarter of an hour. But the defences remained supreme to the end.

The football minded Potteries had been waiting 22 years for this League meeting of local rivals. Half an hour before the kick-off the terraces and paddocks were filling up, but it

was a quietly expectant rather than a noisy crowd, although the supporters of the clubs displayed their colours here and there, and the occasional rattle was sounded.

The sky was overcast and seemed to hold threat of rain, but there was little or no wind, and playing conditions at the start were ideal.

While the crowds were assembling they were entertained by the music of the City of Stoke-on-Trent Special Constabulary Band.

There were no changes from the selected sides. Teams:-

STOKE CITY:-
Robertson, Short, McCue, Mountford, Thomson, Sellars, Malkin, Hutton, King, Cairns, Oscroft.

PORT VALE:-
King, Turner, Potts, Mullard, Cheadle, Sproson, Askey, Leake, Hayward, Griffiths, Cunliffe.

REFEREE:-
Mr J.H. Clough, of Bolton.

Stoke, who lost the toss, kicked off towards the Boothen end before a capacity crowd of 47,000.

There was a lively start when, in the first minute, the referee spoke to Potts after he had brought down King when the centre-forward was trying to thread a way through. Mountford took the resulting free kick and Johnny King rose to flash the ball with his head towards goal, but goalkeeper Ray King was on the alert to deal with the situation.

The Vale repulsed Stoke efforts to snatch an early lead and play moved into the City half, where Thomson and McCue held up the visitors progress.

The players on both sides betrayed an obvious nervous tension at the start and the moves quickly petered out.

Stoke, however, were generally more dangerous and Ray King held off the challenge of three men as they moved in to try a shot which passed outside the post.

There was a businesslike look about a City advance which started from McCue and was continued by Oscroft, whose centre was pushed out and snapped up by Malkin. The outside-right, from centre of the field, hit the ball first time with his left foot but Sproson got in the way to intervene and save his goalkeeper from worry.

The Vale gathered some thrust and Robertson was brought into action for the first time. Then Mullard came running under the ball to head it menacingly into the goalmouth, where again Robertson dealt with the situation.

The Vale forwards were well held although Askey came rushing in to loose a fierce drive which rose well over the bar. The combined work of Stoke was generally more to the point.

IT WAS A NEAR THING FOR THE VALE WHEN JOHNNY KING CROSSED THE BALL FROM THE LEFT AND POTTS, CLOSELY CHALLENGED, ALMOST HEADED THROUGH HIS OWN GOAL, THE BALL NARROWLY CLEARING THE BAR.

Neat tackles by Short twice held up the Vale left wing but, trying again, Cunliffe worked his way towards the middle before slipping a pass across to Mullard, who wasted the opportunity by holding the ball too long and losing it in a tackle.

For a time play was centred uneventfully in mid-field until Oscroft burst through and, from 30 yards, tried a drive which flashed inches over the bar. Long high passes which the Vale tried up the middle availed little, for Thomson was generally Hayward's master

in the air. Faulty passing by Cairns cause some of Stoke's movements to break down.

The game carried occasional thrills when forward rushes by both sides looked like finding a way through – once Ray King had difficulty in smothering a back pass from Cheadle – but from a football sense there was not much to stir the enthusiasm of the crowd. In fact at times each team sent its passes to the other side. Practically all the shooting had come from Stoke.

Malkin, again roaming in the middle, cracked in another tremendous drive which Potts countered as he came rushing into the goalmouth. Not to be outdone, the Vale made their best direct attempt through Mullard with a powerful low drive which flashed past the post.

Johnny King needed careful watching and sometimes the thrusts of Stoke had the Vale defenders kicking with more haste than accuracy. The solid play of Thomson allowed the rather straggled efforts of the Vale attack no scope.

Later, however, the City defence were given their hardest test so far when the Vale forwards made their most constructive progress. Leake, left footed, from Cunliffe's pass, put in a shot with a real scoring look. Only a brilliant save from Robertson who dived and pushed the ball round the post with out-stretched hands kept the Vale out. The danger persisted for Stoke, and Cunliffe moved in close to hook the ball narrowly over the bar.

There were several stoppages for free kicks and once the referee took the name of McCue after a tackle on Askey.

About this time the Vale had begun to show a real improvement and in one hectic spell the City goal was under fire. Robertson made another fine save, one handed, at the foot of the post from Cunliffe and Short cleared off the line.

The Stoke supporters had another scare when Robertson fisted a ball from the right but it went into the side net. Stoke came back into the picture just before the interval only to meet with a close defence which allowed no loopholes.

For the greater part of the first half in a game which achieved no distinctions but was always closely and sternly fought, Stoke looked the better side and it would have been no surprise had they gone ahead; but in the quarter of an hour before the interval the Vale seized the initiative for the first time and they too, came very close to scoring.

So far, however, the defences not without a struggle had managed to keep on top.

The second half began very much after the fashion of the first with the Stoke forwards doing the probing and the Vale defence holding them off.

Cheadle, Sproson and Turner crowded out a thrust from the left and then King broke away to the left to stop a ball which Malkin crossed from the right. Askey, with some clever footwork, tried to make progress for the Vale but Leake was not able to place his pass to any useful purpose.

HUTTON TRIED A SHOT WHICH WAS CHARGED DOWN AND, FOLLOWING UP, THIS TIME LANDED THE BALL WELL WIDE OF THE FAR POST.

For the Vale, Cunliffe had a great run right across field to send Stoke defence back to cover their goal. After the ball had hovered about inside the penalty area, he came across to try an over-head kick which, however, was off the target.

Much of the play was of a scrambling character with Stoke doing most of the attacking. Twice they were awarded free kicks outside the penalty area and Ray King had

to go low to hold drives from Malkin and Oscroft.

Stoke continued to shoot whenever they had the opportunity but the close Vale defence allowed few clear views of goal. Quick collaboration between Oscroft and Malkin saw the outside-right, who had crossed into the middle, meet a pass on the volley and King must have seen little of the ball which swept at great speed an inch over the bar.

Mountford and Sellars held the Vale inside forwards in check and for a long time Robertson had little to do.

The light had been extremely bad since the restart and half way through the second half heavy rain swept the ground. About this time the Vale had made one of their rare assaults on the City goal and had forced a corner but it came to nothing.

In approach the City forwards still held the greater threat, but the Vale defence was still having the last say. King punched out coolly and well when there was a rush from a high centre from Malkin.

Cunliffe was a great trier for the Vale racing here and there in an effort to break through the City defence. He nearly succeeded when a ball on the slippery surface deceived Stoke and he tore in from the left to loose a shot which swept across the face of the goal.

Tackles were still vigorous at times, but as time wore on the game began to wear a negative look, with the Vale rarely effective in attack and the more prominent City forwards well held by the dour Vale defence.

In one of Stoke's attacks a shot from Malkin was deflected and left Oscroft with a great chance but he put the ball weakly outside. As in the first half, the Vale again began to blossom late and in the last quarter of an hour gave Stoke some anxious moments.

The lively Cunliffe almost succeeded in putting his side ahead when he cut in to fire in a tremendous cross drive with Robertson – to the relief of the City supporters – magnificently pushing the ball round the post.

Stoke had lost most of the initiative, and the Vale held them with increasing ease and became the more likely prospects for a goal.

The result was justly a draw. It was a dour battle in which the Vale stopped Stoke's victorious march and were the first team to take a point from them, their defence around the king pin of Cheadle was too good for the Stoke forwards.

Curiously enough, although less prominent in attack, the Vale made the most dangerous scoring attempts. King was generally busier in the Vale goal but Robertson had the more difficult saves to make.

4 September 1954

Can Port Vale continue last season's shock assault in Division II?

Promotion from the Third Division to the First Division in successive seasons (1934-35, 1935-36) by Charlton Athletic is among football's greatest feats. Can Port Vale – Northern Section champions and F.A. Cup semi-finalists – continue last season's shock assault to emulate the London club?

In the new season, which begins next week, Port Vale will be returning to the Second Division after a lapse of 18 years and they might be expected to look more upon consolidating their regained status than towards the risks and strains of any further immediate crusading. But the Vale provided some of the major surprises of last season and there is no doubting their serious intent to achieve the premier goal by the quickest route.

While the club intend to retain their successful formula of neither buying nor selling players and maintaining as far as possible a settled team, they will be prepared to meet any emergency that may arise when their test in the higher grade of the League gets under way.

Naturally the club hope and expect to advance along new ground with their own staff and, as the average age of the team is one which leaves room for maturing form and a number of young players are being groomed for their senior debuts, the prospects here support that view.

If the club had accepted offers made for their players last season, they could have paid for the Vale Park Stadium – with its splendid new stand – all over again and several of the players concerned ought to find in the Second Division new scope for translating their talents into growing renown.

Previewing against the backcloth of last season's triumphal march, a campaign that must now be fought in more select class is a precarious task but faith must be put in the comparative youthfulness of the Vale side (as against the wearing nucleus that failed to keep Oldham Athletic afloat).

Bristol Rovers receive the Vale in the opening game and, as the Vale well know from Southern Section visits to the Eastville Stadium, it will be a tough start. Rovers finished just over half-way last season and if the Vale can find some reward from this initial bout then they will be off to an encouraging start.

And why not? Though eight Second Division clubs scored more goals than the Vale last season – and the Vale may have to watch this aspect more closely than last time – no Second Division team could better the Vale's 16 victories and no defeats at home.

Of course, the Vale, in setting up a new defensive record, had the fewest goals against in the whole of the League. They conceded only five at home and the nearest to this in the Second Division was the 16 of Blackburn, who missed promotion by a point.

In away games, the Vale's 16 goals against record was better by far than any in the Second Division where the lowest was 31 by Everton, one of the two clubs promoted to the First Division.

Strength that the Vale should be able to meet the Second Division challenge also comes from their Cup conquests that season over First Division Cardiff City (away) and Blackpool (at Vale Park) and in their performance against West Bromwich Albion in the semi-final at Villa Park.

Mention of those illustrious opponents quickly freshens the mind and, with play of that calibre and spirit, who can think otherwise than that the Vale are on the threshold of their greatest days?

It is not so much the first home match – against Notts County on the evening of Monday August 23rd – that supporters will eagerly await as the third away fixture of the season which takes them to the Victoria Ground for the first derby of the season with Stoke City. It is the match that all the Potteries will want to see. The next away game is due to be played at Doncaster and this may be switched from the Saturday to the Monday to avoid a clash with the St Leger attraction and traffic.

Christmas this year will be spent in an exchange with Fulham and the New Year will

be greeted at Plymouth. Easter will be shared with Liverpool, with a trip to Middlesbrough in between.

The curtain will rise on a cast that attracted a much increased following last season under loyal captain Tom Cheadle. The Vale should have no fears in defence and at half-back they will have Mullard's experience and wholehearted play and natural skill of Sproson.

Leake has already served the team with a utility and effectiveness that makes him a valued asset and whatever becomes his major role in the new season, he can be relied upon again to give excellent service.

Leake was in the Vale's leading trio of scorers, the others being vigorous leader Hayward and inside-left Griffiths.

In Cunliffe the Vale have a stocky, plucky outside-left and in Askey an outside-right who can rise to great heights at times.

With Tomkinson making his debut last season and Bennett returning after illness, the Vale should find ready reserve strength at hand and this applies also to the rearguard where Elsby (on several occasions) and Brien (in one appearance) last season showed their value.

The playing staff is:-

PROFESSIONALS:

Full time --- Askey, Barber, Bould, Brien, Burrows, Cheadle, Conway, Cunliffe, Elsby, Fitzgerald, Griffiths, Hancock, Hayward, Hulligan King, Leake, Mountford, Mullard, Potts, Rowe, Sproson, Tomkinson, Turner, Willdigg, Higgs, Moran, Austin, Donaldson, Bennett.
Part Time --- Finney, Oliver.

AMATEURS:

Goalkeepers: D.H.Bowd, Buffey, D. Cooper, F.Follows.
Full-backs: G. Craig, F. Davies, W. McMillan, G.Steadman, W.Tams, T.Whitehall.
Half-backs: G.G. Allen, A. Elsmore, J.H. Fieldhouse, D. Goodwin, T.Miles, R. Mountford, A. Price, D.T. Smith, T. Taylor, C.E. Worrall, G.H. Wallbanks.
Forwards: R.G. Askev, R. Alcock, G. Barnett, P. Beardmore, D.J. Cumberbatch, H. Davies, B. Dobson, J. Dorrien, A. Ford, K. Fullwood, F.A. Hough, J. Massey, C. Mosley, J. Pierpoint, J. Robinson, J. Reeves, S.F. Steele, A.G. Simmill, D. Welch.

12 August 1954

Port Vale full-back Jim Elsby played for the club from 1949 to 1955.

Roy Sproson's memorable matches and 'unfriendly' friendlies!

Two League games I particularly recall were at Tranmere and Gateshead. At Gateshead they had been used to small gates; in fact, there were about 1,700 the week before we played there but when Vale hit town 18,000 turned out to watch us.

At Tranmere we were clapped onto the park because of what we had done for the Third Division in reaching the FA Cup semi-finals, yet after beating Tranmere 4-0 those same people threw bricks, bottles and anything they could get their hands on at us.

After the 1953-54 promotion season we went on a tour of Ireland and there we became involved in what I call the "Battle of Cork." We had previously beaten a Representative XI 4-0 in Dublin and animosity was stacked against us.

7 - 1 THRASHING

Nevertheless, Manager Freddie Steele instructed us to take it easy until the home side started to kick chunks out of us in the first half and led 1-0 at half-time. I had my eye split.

Freddie then told us "let 'em have it" and they hardly knew what had hit them. They had bitten off more than they could chew and we won 4-1 in the end.

During our Second Division days I was unfortunate enough to be part of one of the biggest home trouncing Port Vale have suffered.

Some fans will know the game I am referring to... a 7-1 thrashing by Nottingham Forest. Mastermind that day was Eddie Baily, who had moved from Vale to Forest that season. Stuart Imlach had a field day and I ran my legs off trying to mark a winger called Barrett.

Forest were promoted that season and we were relegated. After that particular match, we waited until it was dark before going home and dared not set foot outside the house all day Sunday.

Another cup-tie I will long remember was at Sunderland where we gained a goalless draw. On the Friday night we went to a local cinema to see a film called "Town without Pity," and the papers told us the next day that that was how we would find Sunderland.

The papers paired the players in direct opposition and gave their verdict.

I was against Harry Hooper and was given "no chance" as were many of our lads but I talked Hooper out of the game.

I knew he was not particularly brave and told him I was going to put him over the stand. He was frightened to death.

We had some luck in that game, like the moment when a shot by Herd beat Ken Hancock in goal only to hit me on the knee and go clear in the first minute.

But Hancock was great that day, performing the best save I have ever seen in the dying moments.

He broke his ankle in the first few minutes of the return but stayed on as we won 3-1. Colin Grainger, once of Sunderland, took them apart that night.

Often in football eight or nine lads in the team will hit peak form together but seldom do all 11. I was proud to be part of a Vale team when every man struck gold.

That was in a match at Grimsby where we won 5-0 and none of us wanted to hear the final whistle. We had three goals disallowed.

We took a drubbing for the first 20 minutes and then started to play and I mean play. The referee was Jack Kelley and it was his last match.

Afterwards he told us it was one of the best he had ever seen and I was fortunate to take part in one of the best constructed goals I can ever remember.

Ten Vale players touched the ball before Dennis Fidler put it into the net. It was poetic and we were cheered off by the home crowd.

FARCICAL MATCH

I have mentioned one memorable experience on tour and another I will never forget occurred in Poland in the early 1960s. After drawing 1-1 with the Polish champions, Polonia, we were up against an Army team before a 30,000 crowd.

The match was farcical and ended some 20 minutes from time when the entire Port Vale team was sent off.

The referee was so biased it was ridiculous and the flashpoint happened when Stan Steele became involved in an incident.

Stan, short and stocky, could hardly be mistaken but the referee dismissed Peter Ford, who bore no resemblance to Stan whatsoever.

Peter rightly refused to go and in an attempt to sort out the chaos and interpreter came onto the pitch with Norman Low.

Norman told us to line up in our normal positions while the discussions went on and finally the referee pointed to all of us in turn and signalled to the dressing room. That was the only time I have ever been sent off.

During the later stages of my career the game I recall most was at Scunthorpe in the 1969-70 promotion campaign. We had gone our first 18 games

without defeat and one more would have given us a record. Instead we lost 3-2 and I gave away a penalty and an own goal.

NOT TO BLAME

The game, which many still talk about, is the game I did not play. That was League game number 765 which would have broken Jimmy Dickinson's record for appearances for a single club, in his case, Portsmouth.

I have heard many people hold Gordon Lee to blame for this. Why did he not give me those extra games? I was being asked.

The truth is that had it not been for Gordon Lee I would never have been anywhere near Dickinson's achievement by the time I had packed up. Also, had I not missed a chunk of 1958-59 season with an ankle injury, I would have reached the milestone.

It should be remembered that for three seasons running Gordon Lee talked me out of retirement. I eventually played over 100 games for him otherwise the record would have been out of the question. That I did not beat it never bothered me at all.

3 March 1975

Basil Haywood, once a policeman, also played as centre-forward for Port Vale.

Female spectators show their support for Vale.

Jackie Mudie leaves the A&E hospital after a car crash. Seen with him from left to right is: Len Barker (Director), Reg Berks (Chief Scout) and Arthur McPherson (Chairman). Reg Berks became Chief Scout for Vale in 1965. He left Vale for a time and became a publican but returned in 1974 as the Coach and Chief Scout.

Seen in action is former Port Vale players Harry Poole. Poole played for Vale between 1956 and 1968. Poole was extremely skilled and whilst at Vale he played in various pitch positions including wing-half, inside-forward and centre-forward.

Griffiths on the "list" — own request

Ken Griffiths, the Port Vale inside forward, has been put on the transfer list at his own request. The Vale Board agreed to Griffiths's request for a transfer at a meeting last night. Mr Fred Steele, the Vale Manager, said today: "The player thinks that a change of club will be beneficial to him."

A native of Abbey Hulton, Griffiths has made nearly 200 appearances for the Vale's first team. He began as a goalkeeper and became an inside forward while in the R.A.F. He made his League debut for the Vale in the 1949-50 season.

Griffiths was a regular member of the Vale's promotion-winning side and he also took part in the Vale's memorable Cup run but, unfortunately, missed the semi-final through injury. Griffiths has been unable to get a regular place in the Vale's League side this season, having made only six appearances.

27 November 1956

Vale's Ken Griffiths moves to Mansfield

Ken Griffiths, Port Vale's inside-forward, will sign for Mansfield Town late this afternoon and will be in their team to play Accrington Stanley at home tomorrow.

Terms were agreed between the two clubs after Griffiths and the Vale Manager, Mr Norman Low, had visited Mansfield today to complete the signature. The fee is well in the four figure class.

PRESSING NEED

Mansfield are hoping that Griffiths, who scored two magnificent goals in the Vale's Cheshire League game against Runcorn last Saturday, will solve their pressing need for a forward. His position tomorrow is his normal one, inside-left.

Mansfield still have an outside chance of promotion and they think Griffiths' arrival may keep alive their hopes. Griffiths is the latest of the Vale's celebrated promotion side to leave the club. He helped to take the team to the FA Cup semi-final in the same season, but had to miss the big match because of injury. He has made only three first team appearances this season.

24 January 1958

Ray King renews transfer request

The position of Ray King, Port Vale's goalkeeper, is to be discussed again by the Board of Directors soon.

King who is worried about the health of his five-years-old son, had a talk with the Manager, Mr Fred Steele, today about the prospects of a move from Vale Park to a climate which might be better for his son.

He is hoping that the Vale Board will reconsider the request he made at the beginning of this season for a move. The Vale chairman (Mr F. W. Burgess) said after the Board had first discussed King's request that, although they had reluctantly refused, it might be possible for them to reconsider it at a later date.

King told the Sentinel today: "I am getting desperate about the boy's health. It is not improving and a move seems the only way out."

22 October 1956

Vale transfer Ray King to Boston United

Port Vale goalkeeper Ray King, who was recently offered terms by the club, was last night transferred to Boston United, the Midland League club. He is to be their player-manager.

The fee is not disclosed, but is believed to be between £2,000 and £3,000. The deal was completed after two officials from Boston had travelled to Burslem to meet the player and members of the Vale Board.

King is the last of the Vale's famous defensive trio to leave Vale Park, Turner and Potts having previously joined Southern League Club Worcester City. He was originally on the transfer list but was later asked to re-sign.

King joined the Vale in 1949, having previously been with Leyton Orient and Newcastle United. He made well over 200 League appearances for the Vale. In 1954 he gained England "B" honours and last year toured South Africa with the FA party.

The Vale manager, Mr Norman Low, said today that he would try and fill the vacancy before next season opens.

5 July 1957

Ray King England XI. Reserve –to travel to Belgrade.

Ray King, the Port Vale goalkeeper, is to travel as reserve for the full England side which meets Jugoslavia in Belgrade on May 16th.

Also in reserve will be Bill McGarry, the Huddersfield Town and former Vale wing-half. Should England's new centre-half Owen, of Luton Town, not satisfy requirements, McGarry may be brought in at right-half if Wright, the England captain is switched to centre-half for the second match against Hungary in Budapest on May 23rd.

Owen in place of Clarke (Tottenham Hotspurs) is the only change from the England side which defeated Scotland 4-2 at Hampden Park on April 3rd. Owen's inclusion is another of many experiments to try and solve a position that has been a big England problem since Neil Franklin's days.

Ron Allen of West Bromwich Albion, who was formerly with the Vale, again leads the England attack, and the team will be:-

Merrick (Birmingham)
Staniforth (Huddersfield)
Byrne (Manchester United)
Wright (Wolverhampton captain)
Owen (Luton)
Dickinson (Portsmouth)
Finney (Preston)
Broadis (Newcastle)
Allen (West Bromwich)
Nicholls (West Bromwich)
Mullen (Wolverhampton)

Reserves travelling with the team:

King (Port Vale)
McGarry (Huddersfield)
Harris (Portsmouth)
Sewell (Sheffield Wednesday)

The England "B" team to play Jugoslavia "B" at Ljubljana, also on May 16th will be:-

Burgin (Sheffield Wednesday)
Green (Birmingham)
Mansell (Portsmouth)
Armstrong (Chelsea captain)
Dugdale (West Bromwich)
Bell (Bolton)
Hooper (West Ham)
Quixall (Sheffield Wednesday)
Jezzard (Fulham)
Haynes (Fulham)
Robb (Tottenham)

Travelling with the "B" team will be:

Thompson (Preston)
Edwards (Manchester United)
Wilshaw (Wolverhampton)

11 May 1954

Terry Miles, local lad, was a regular player in the 1958-59 promotion side and in the 1960-61 team. He made 401 appearance for Vale and scored 17 goals. Miles became the first playing substitute for Port Vale in 1965.

John Poole graduated through Vale's juniors and signed as a 'pro' in September 1953. He made his debut as keeper in a 3-2 home win against Middlesbrough on the 28 April 1956. Poole was used as a reserve until November 1959 when he became a regular on the first team. He lost his place after a 6-3 defeat at Mansfield Town where he fractured his nose. He moved to Macclesfield Town in May 1961 when he was given a free transfer.

A storming finale by Port Vale

Port Vale have won the Fourth Division Championship and no theatrical producer could have put on a better finale to the season than they did last night in beating Millwall 5-2 at Vale Park.

The grand climax came after the match when 3,000 spectators waited for the Vale Manager, Mr Norman Low, the players and the directors to appear on the balcony of the directors' box. They did so and the Vale skipper, Albert Leake, flanked by his victorious team-mates, thanked the fans for their support during the season. It was a happy ending to an extremely arduous season.

The 13,473 spectators saw the Vale, in driving rain, play like champions to open up a 2-0 lead. They lost their poise temporarily to allow Millwall to draw level, and then, spurred on by the loud-speaker announcement that Coventry had lost at Hartlepool, come back with a great three-goal finish that sent the crowd wild.

The Vale have rarely played better and might easily have scored more. Playing in their new kit, which has rather more of an orange tint than the old amber, the Vale quickly showed that they were not to be put off by the seriousness of the occasion.

IN THE MUD

Both Steele and Barnett might have netted in the opening minutes and a strong Poole shot, partially stopped by goalkeeper Davies, stuck in the mud an inch or two from the goal-line. Not that Millwall were inactive, Crowshaw broke away to drive outside and veteran Ackerman emerged from a pack of players to shoot over.

The Vale's first goal, after 17 minutes, followed a move started by Steele, whose pass was touched forward by Poole to Barnett, who ran through, drew the Millwall goalkeeper ad found the net with a well-placed ground shot. Goalkeeper Davies was kept busy for some time afterwards – one diving save from Cunliffe must be mentioned – before

Barnett beat him again, after 31 minutes, with a fine header from Cunliffe's perfect centre.

Millwall, though, had been plugging away for some time when Dawson made it 2-1 with a good header from a free kick taken near the corner flag. For a time afterwards the Vale's prestige was in danger, particularly when Ackerman scored a good equaliser 10 minutes after the interval. But there was no stopping the Vale in the last 20 minutes. They scored three times and only the mud and some desperate goalkeeping by Davies kept the score down to reasonable limits.

Poole headed in No. 3 from Jackson's centre after 65 minutes; Jackson himself followed with the fourth – a shot from the by-line which hit a post before the ball entered the net – three minutes later; and Cunliffe rounded off the evening with the fifth, after twice beating right-back Redmond.

Barnett missed his hat-trick by inches – a header of his hit the top of the bar – but the unluckiest Vale player was Steele, the only forward not to score when one goal would have given him the club's scoring record in post-war football. There was not a weakness in this Vale team, and it would be indivious to single out any one player.

On this performance the club can approach next season with the greatest optimism.

PORT VALE:-
Hancock, Raine, Sproson, Kinsey, Leake, Miles, Jackson, Steele, Poole, Barnett, Cunliffe.

MILLWALL:-
Davies, Redmond, Brady, White, Harper, Vaessen, Broadfoot, Ackerman, Moyse, Rawson, Crowshaw.

REFEREE:-
Mr R. A. Windle, of Chesterfield.

28 April 1959

Roy Sproson looks back at Vale's men at the top.

UPS AND DOWNS – WITH SEVEN MANAGERS

In my 22 years as a player at Vale Park, I served under seven managers. The first I encountered was the late Gordon Hodgson and the last was Gordon Lee. Of them all, I think Norman Low was the most memorable.

The tragic death of Gordon Hodgson was, I recall, a shattering blow to the club and particularly the younger players like myself whom he had signed.

I had played for Trent Vale against Port Vale in the Sentinel Shield. We won 5-0 and Gordon Hodgson came and presented us with a strip. I also played a couple of games for Stoke City 'A' and was told that they would sign me when I came out of the Forces. Instead, Vale were prepared to sign me there and then before I enlisted and I received £3 a week during my National Service.

On my demob, I played for Vale as a part-timer for a spell. I began in the Staffs County League progressed to the Cheshire League and then made my league debut at Gillingham on November 11th 1950... all in the space of a couple of months.

I was part of Vale's youth policy and Mr Hodgson was responsible for blooding most of the team who later reached the FA Cup semi-finals and gained promotion.

Gordon Hodgson was a fair chap. He would give you a rollicking one minute and then it would be forgotten. Everybody liked and respected him and his loss was so sad. He went into hospital at the end of the 1950-51 season and I never saw him again, although he left Vale with a good staff and one destined to go places.

KNEE INJURY

My second manager after Mr Hodgson was Ivor Powell, who arrived as player-manager when getting over a knee injury sustained with Aston Villa. Ivor never seemed to regain full fitness and everything seemed to go wrong for him at Vale.

He was not particularly liked. He used to treat the players as kids and I had the impression that older pros, in particular, resented him. It was not a surprise that he did not last long.

One player-manager succeeded another when Freddie Steele took over on leaving Mansfield. The immediate effect was that the younger players went out of the side in favour of the more senior professionals.

We had the occasional game, but generally Freddie looked to experience and did well as the club finished halfway in the old Third Division (South).

RUNNERS-UP

The next term (1952-53) we were transferred to the Third (North) and the youngsters had more of a look-in. I played in all 46 games and we finished runners-up to Oldham, missing promotion by two points.

But things were beginning to happen. Freddie was a great psychologist. He was also a tremendous tactician and, looking back, was years ahead of his time.

We were playing 4-2-4 in 1953 before anyone ever labelled it as such and, as a left-half, I was operating then what is now referred to as a double centre-half.

FIVE YEARS

Those were the days of the so-called "iron curtain" defence and Freddie was like a Svengali to us. But he would get tensed up himself. There were times when, if we were drawing or winning a tight Cup game, Freddie would disappear for the last five minutes and was to be found hiding in the toilet.

Freddie had some five years at Vale but, in 1957, the club paid the penalty for not strengthening an under-staffed squad and we came down back to the Third (South).

So Freddie went and Norman Low arrived. He was a man who created a great impression on me and it was during Norman's stay with the Club that Port Vale played, to my mind, the best football in my time.

The reason was Norman's insistence on attacking play. He is the only manager I have ever heard tell his team to go out and entertain the public. Norman would never discuss the opposition and he would rollick us for winning only 1-0 when the score should have been 6-5.

Some of Norman's beliefs would make today's managers shudder. He would not tolerate defensive play at any price and would not hear of going away for a point. As a result we used to win games 6-4, 5-3 and 5-0 and, for the first time since I became a pro, we were never in danger of any relegation.

LEAN SPELL

For a spell in Norman's first season (1957-58), we led the Third (South), but hit a lean spell and eventually finished 15th. A season later, we romped away with the newly formed Fourth Division, cracking home 110 goals in the process.

It was one of the biggest mysteries to me why Norman was sacked at a time when we were sixth from top of the Third Division. He called me into his office and said: "I have just been fired. I have been let down by some of the players."

The news came as a tremendous surprise and a

shock because, to me, Norman was a most likeable man and with more contacts in football than anyone I have known.

The departure of Norman Low – he went to Liverpool as chief scout – heralded the return of Freddie Steele, who had been out of the game. He was working locally when recalled to Vale Park and the decision rather surprised us.

CUP EPICS

I felt that Fred had changed when he came back. He had not got the same enthusiasm and drive as before, but he did have something, because the lads still responded to him ad we enjoyed some Cup epics – against Liverpool and Birmingham, for example.

Fred left again in the 1964-65 season and Jackie Mudie arrived as player-manager after we had been relegated to the Fourth Division. It was at this stage that the whole club changed.

Sir Stanley Matthews joined as General Manager with Jackie Mudie and the expensive policy of bringing "wonder boys" down from the North-East and all over began. To my mind, the club had their priorities wrong and, as a result, the first team suffered badly.

Attempts to launch a youth policy were being made while the League team were being ignored and Stan, charming man that he was, suffered from being misinformed.

CLUB SLIDING

He trusted people who should never have been trusted and people took advantage of him. I am convinced a lot of people sponged off him and all the while the club were sliding.

We just avoided having to seek re-election in 1967-68 but were expelled anyway for alleged illegal payments. The club was really in a sorry state.

I was 38 and, as a player, I had had enough. It was only the arrival of Gordon Lee in 1968 that revived my career. I told him I wanted to finish but he maintained that I could "still be useful" and persuaded me to carry on a little longer.

I was not in the side to start with but after a few games I came back to form a partnership with Johnny King. We had a strong defence and got what we could up front and, at the end of the season (1968-1969), had done well to finish half-way.

We felt that we could even achieve something and, sure enough, gained promotion the following season.

Gordon Lee was a great person to work for. He was straight as a die but, if anything, rather cautious and predictable. If he took over a team in North Vietnam, I would know the way they play. Yet, he played according to the players he had at his disposal, even though he was often criticised for being negative.

Without Gordon Lee, I do not know where Port Vale would be today. He was a brave man in taking the job and put life back into the club for others to reap the benefit in the more prosperous days of today.

17 February 1975

Despite finishing the season just below half-way in the Third Division, Vale did have a profitable FA Cup run, defeating Queen's Park Rangers, Cardiff City and Scunthorpe United before bowing out 2-1 to Aston Villa on 20 February 1960, in front of 49,768 fans at Vale Park. Port Vale 1959-60 season team shot.

Norman Low took over as manager of Vale from Freddie Steele in February 1957, having already had spells in charge at Norwich City and Workington Town.

Chapter 4
1960-1965

By the start of the Sixties Port Vale were back in the Third Division under the management of Norman Low. Low lost no time at all in signing new players and a revitalised Vale emerged with a satisfying blend of old and new team members.

Vale made it through to the Fifth Round of the FA Cup in the 1959-60 season and saw the highest ever attendance at Vale Park of 49,768 fans. The Valiants were unlucky and lost to Aston Villa 1-2. A lacklustre performance in the rest of the season saw Vale placed 14th in the Third Division league tables.

In May 1960 Vale took a friendly tour of Czechoslovakia playing five matches in total. The Czechoslovakian national team were so impressed by Vale's attitude and excitement to the game that they agreed to play a friendly the following year.

The early 1960s saw Port Vale remain steadily in the middle of Division Three with no real progression. After only a few months into the 1962-63 season Norman Low made a surprise departure from Vale, apparently due to a disagreement with the club's board of directors. The new manager was a surprise to fans and players alike, Mr Freddie Steele after a five year absence was invited back.

Freddie Steele made no secret of the fact that it was his intention to invest in a strong youth policy at Vale. Yet true to form Steele also secured well seasoned players like Jackie Mudie, from rivals Stoke City. Once again Vale's 'Iron Curtain' manager was trying to create a well balanced side of new and experienced players in order to boost Vale back as a contender for promotion.

Unfortunately after a disastrous 1962-63 season Steele resigned and left Vale Park for the last time. He was replaced by player-manager Jackie Mudie who in turn passed the mantle of managerial responsibility onto his long-time friend Sir Stanley Matthews. Although Vale were bottom of the Third Division in the 1964-65 season, the partnership of Mudie and Matthews inspired confidence in players and fans alike.

As the 1960-61 season approached manager Norman Low was able to strengthen Vale with three new signings. Ted Calland from Exeter City, Dennis Fidler from Manchester City and John Bailey from Northwich Victoria. The board, anxious to see Vale progress, made funds available to Low to sign the right players. Aston Villa were approached regarding Gerry Hitchens, who was ranked as one of the League's top centre-forwards, and definite efforts were made to sign Bert Llewellyn from Crewe Alexandra. There was even speculation that Ronnie Allen would soon return to Vale. Pictured left to right: Norman Low (Manager), Lot Hamlett (Trainer) and Ted Calland (centre-forward).

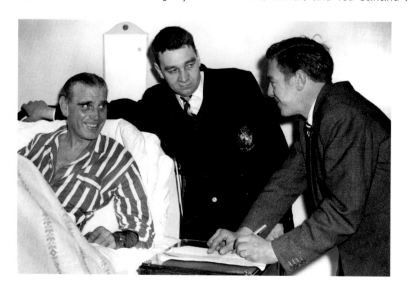

While still in his hospital bed after an operation on his Achilles tendon, Manager Norman Low still manages to sign on Ralph Hunt (formerly Swindon Town) to play for Vale. Club director Arthur McPherson, pictured centre, witnesses the transfer.

Dennis Fidler
joined Vale from
Manchester City
in August 1960.

Goalkeeper John Cooke
worked his way through
the junior ranks of Port
Vale to become a member
of the first team in 1960.
He made 7 appearances
for Vale before he left the
club in 1964.

One that got away. John Poole in action in October 1960.

Vale's squad for the opening of the 1960-61 season.

Top row left to right: Selwyn Whalley, Dennis Fidler, Ted Calland, Peter Ford, Harry Poole, Graham Barnett.

Second row: Roy Gater, Peter Hall, John Poole, Ken Hancock, Roy Sproson, Terry Lowe.

Third row: Terry Miles, Cliff Portwood, Norman Low (manager), Albert Leake, John Archer, David Raine.

Bottom row: Noel Kinsey, Stan Steele, Barry Hancock, Colin Davies, Brian Jackson.

Using football clubs and individual players in advertising has always added extra revenue streams to the club and player's coffers, however, endorsing products as wholesome as milk seem to be a thing of the past. Also advertised here are the costs for season ticket holders in the 1960-61 season – if only these prices still applied!!

October 1961 and three young newcomers played a big part in Vale's 2-1 victory over Reading. Left to right: Derek Edge, Roy Gater and Stan Edwards.

John Nicholson signed for Vale from Liverpool for £2,000 in August 1961. The 24 year old full-back had been with Liverpool since he was a boy but he made only a handful of first team appearances, though he did captain their Central League side during the 1959-60 and 1960-61 seasons. Nicholson had already agreed terms with Crewe Alexandra but then decided he liked Vale better.

Pictured here are the visiting Czechoslavakian team of 1961. They played a friendly match with Port Vale prior to their World Cup qualifying match against the Republic of Ireland. Vale Park attracted a crowd of over 22,000, but the Czech national team proved their superior talent in a 3-1 victory.

Joining Port Vale in the 1961-62 season from Middlesbrough, Peter Taylor only ever played as goalkeeper for the Valiants once before being transferred to Burton Albion.

Seen together are Mike Porter and Terry Lowe. Mike Porter signed as a professional footballer for Vale in July 1962. He made his debut against Barnsley in April 1964. He never became a regular on the team and was finally given a free transfer in 1965. Terry Lowe started his career playing for Stoke City before joining Vale in 1960. He made his debut as right-back in a 1-0 win at Stoke City in the Supporters' Club's Trophy final on 24 April 1961.

New Vale manager's plan to foster local talent

So Freddie Steele, 45-years-old former Stoke City and England star, steps back into football as Manager of Port Vale the club he quit five years ago.

The news, which came only a few hours after the announcement of Norman Low's resignation, is the biggest bombshell to have exploded on the Vale Park scene in years. Vale's appointment not only turns the clock back five years when Low succeeded Steele in the Manager's chair.

It presents the most intriguing poser about Vale's future at a time when the club's reputation has been badly tarnished by a disappointing start to the season.

Can a man of proven Soccer ability and experience successfully take up the club reins after five years out of the game? Vale think Mr Steele can and will.

Says the club Chairman Mr Joe Machin: "We feel he will never forget his experience as a player and a manager. And we are sure that he will take Vale back into the Second Division."

High hopes indeed but no-one can deny that Steele guided the Burslem side to halcyon days in their history. That fight into the semi-final of the FA Cup and promotion to the Second Division are still golden memories.

Can it be done? Over to the new manager.

KEYSTONES

One of the keystones of his policy will be to do all he can to foster local soccer talent. "The policy is fundamentally as good as any. It is easy enough to spend money on ready-made players but, at the same time, I am convinced that a lot of football talent can be attracted from the district," he told me this week.

The manager hopes that everyone interested in the welfare of Port Vale will act as the club's unofficial "eyes and ears."

"If they see anyone who would benefit the club I should like to be the first to know of him" says.

Finally, will Freddie Steele's return to a Vale Park mean the return of that famous "Steele Curtain" defence?

The new manager explodes that one right away. "At no time during my previous association with Vale was a direct defensive policy pursued," he says." The reputation of that famous Burslem side sprang from the excellence of the defence, Press "label" and the fact that the opposition were almost always trying to stop Vale scoring."

Over to Mr Low. He has not by any stretch of the imagination had an easy passage at Vale Park. Managers are often the whipping stock for things beyond their control and everyone who knows the co-operative, likeable Norman Low will wish him the best of luck in this most insecure profession in the world.

3 November 1962

Make way for Vale's naval officer!

from platform four, sir."

"I was completely bewildered until it dawned on me that the driver was wearing a Royal Navy cap and had obviously mistaken me for a naval V.I.P. he had been told to pick up," grinned Freddie today. "What happened to the real passenger I hesitate to think." The Vale Manager, who was wearing a long black naval style overcoat, was making the journey to Kent to inspect the Gillingham ground before Wednesday's Cup-tie.

26 January 1963

Port Vale Manager Freddie Steele had an extraordinary taxi ride across London yesterday.

Arriving at Euston Station on the first leg of the trip to Gillingham, he was promptly ushered into a cab by a uniformed chauffeur, driven smartly to Waterloo Station, and saluted as he climbed out of the vehicle. The driver refused Mr Steele's proffered fare, and left with the remark: "Your train for Chatham leaves

Port Vale clinch Benfica match coup

Port Vale have pulled off one of the biggest sporting coups of the year by arranging to stage a game against European Cup-holders Benfica at Vale Park in September.

The game, which will cost Vale a guarantee in the region of £10,000, will be played on the evening of Thursday, September 12th, and it is believed that Benfica will be flying to this country to fulfil this one fixture.

The man behind the coup, which represents a tremendous feat for a Third Division side, is Vale Manager Freddie Steele, who has been in close contact with Benfica's sole agent in this country.

Benfica, the Lisbon side who have won the European Cup for the last two years and are again in the semi-finals this time, are pledged to play their full-strength side, which includes the great Eusebio.

The game has been arranged predominantly as a big Soccer occasion to put before the supporters and not as a profit-making venture, Mr Steele stressed today.

"If the guarantee is met we will be happy," says Mr Steele, who adds: "The match will be the forerunner of others involving internationally-known teams which will be staged at Vale Park as part of a progressive policy."

The game, which will be staged shortly after the start of the new season, will obviously prompt the club Board to consider ground improvements during the summer. Details of ticket prices and reservations will be made known in good time.

A visit by Benfica to an English First Division side is rare enough. A visit to a Third Division club is unknown and Vale can feel well pleased with their feat.

5 April 1963

The season ended with promotion to the Second Division for Palace and Coventry City while Port Vale finished in the middle of the table on a comfortable 46 points having played 46, won 16, drawn 14, and lost 16. The following season Vale collapsed, amassing only 32 points out of a possible 92 and were relegated to the basements along with Colchester and Barnsley. Ken Hancock, pictured here in the game against Crystal Palace in 1963, played for Stoke City before joining Vale as an amateur in 1958. He made his debut as keeper in a 4-2 defeat at Milwall on 13 December 1958.

Mudie and Wilson "Package" Deal

Port Vale this afternoon signed Stoke City's Scottish international forward Jackie Mudie and reserve full-back Ron Wilson for a "package" fee of between £12,000 and £15,000.

The two clubs got together after last night's meeting of the Stoke Board and negotiations, which seemed to have reached deadlock in regard to Mudie a week ago, were reopened. Terms were agreed this morning. Stoke Manager Tony Waddington said:

" This is one of those deals which is of benefit for both clubs and players concerned. Jackie Mudie has played extremely well for us and we will be sorry to lose him. But the overriding factor in the transfer is that the move will probably be of advantage to both players. As Tony Allen's understudy, Ron Wilson was not likely to have normal scope in furthering his playing career here. No pressure was brought to bear on either player and it was left to them to make the choice. We would have been happy if they had chosen to remain."

Vale's need of "wee Jackie," who can play in any of the inside forward positions, has, of course, increased since inside-left Albert Cheesebrough was told this week about the need for a cartilage operation which should keep him out of the game for some weeks.

Wilson will get the left-back spot in Vale's side allowing evergreen Roy Sproson to move up to wing-half. Neither player will be available for tomorrow's game at Bradford because of the Cup deadline requirements, but both will be ready to step into the side for next week's home game against Colchester.

15 November 1963

Superstition delays Vale transfer

Superstition and Soccer are no strangers, so yesterday's transfer deal between Stoke City and Port Vale became today's signings, watched by Mr Tom Talbot (Chairman), Mr Freddie Steele (Manager) and Alderman F. W. Burgess (Director).

Jack Mudie and Ron Wilson agreed yesterday to join Port Vale, but the transfer forms were not completed at Vale Park until this morning, just before the two players set out with their new colleagues to watch the Cup-tie at Bradford City.

Jackie Mudie, a player taught by Soccer experience not to court bad luck, believes in avoiding Friday signings if possible, even if it is not the 13th. Manager Steele, who certainly does not like tempting fate, prefers to leave the signing until the day after agreement has been reached between the clubs and with the players.

So, officially, Mudie and Wilson did not become Vale players until this morning. There was no hurry of course, since they could not be signed in time to play in today's Cup-tie, otherwise superstition may well have had to take a back seat.

16 November 1963

Billy Bingham joined Vale from League Champions Everton at the end of the 1962-63 season, for a then equal club record fee of £15,000. Unfortunately, his playing career was cut short when he broke his leg in a 4-0 defeat at Brentford on 5 September 1964. After receiving a free transfer he joined Southport as manager.

Signed from Nottingham
Forest in 1962 for £6,000,
John Rowland became Port
Vale's top scorer in the 1965-
66 season. He made 166
appearances and scored 43
goals in total before he was
sold on to Mansfield Town for
£6,500.

Taken in the early 60s, full-back Terry Lowe (left) and winger John
Rowland (right).

Port Vale team picture from August 1963 featuring players like Terry Lowe, Terry Alcock, Dennis Fidler, Stan Edwards and John Cooke as goalkeeper.

Action at Workington as Vale's centre-half John Nicholson aided and abetted by Selwyn Whalley robs the Reds' forward Dave Carr.

Albert Cheeseborough signed for Vale from Leicester City for £15,000. Between 1963 to 1966 he appeared 59 times and scored 14 goals for the Valiants.

In the 1964-65 season Terry Alcock played 28 matches as a right-back before switching positions to centre-half. He left Port Vale for Blackpool two seasons later but rejoined Vale in 1977. Alcock finished his league career at Halifax Town after being unable to agree satisfactory terms with the board at Vale.

David Mitchell progressed through Vale's junior ranks and played for the club from 1964-1966. He scored a total of 5 goals at Vale and made in total 24 appearances.

Is this a new form of exercise for the Port Vale team? Some members look a little more convinced than others!

Brilliant Vale hold favourites – goalless draw – and they almost won

52,000 crowd see defence dampen Liverpool fire

LIVERPOOL 0
PORT VALE 0

In Port Vale's great Cup history, few of their performances have lived up to this one. Vale, tipped for a whipping by everyone outside the Potteries, claimed the highest accolade of Anfield this afternoon as the partisan home crowd rose to salute their feat. For three-quarters of the game, Vale, playing with tremendous skill and enthusiasm, had the edge on one of the most dangerous teams in the land. Then Jackie Mudie, whose inspiration was the talk of Liverpool, was injured – but Vale still held out.

It was one of the great moments of Vale's Cup history as the Potteries lads stepped out under the eyes of a madly-enthusiastic 52,000 Anfield crowd to take on the Cup favourites in this fourth round tie. It was an awesome sight for the several thousand Vale fans as the famous Kop swayed and roared their Merseyside chants. But the Potteries team, embarking on their 24th Cup battle in five seasons, were undaunted as their biggest following for 10 years gave them a huge welcome.

Manager Freddie Steele played the same fighting side which had ousted Birmingham

– which meant the exclusion of Billy Bingham and Albert Cheesebrough. For Vale, skipper John Nicholas, stand-in centre-half at Anfield for seven seasons, and winger Ron Smith it was a nostalgic homecoming. But neither had any doubts about their tasks.

Liverpool, studded with internationals, had Ron Yeats back at centre-half after injury.

Teams:

LIVERPOOL,
Lawrence, Thompson, Byrne, Milne, Yeats, Stevenson, Callaghan, Hunt, Arrowsmith, St John, Thompson.

PORT VALE,
Hancock, Whalley, Wilson, Rawlings, Nicholson, Sproson, Rowland, Steele, Richards, Mudie, Smith.

REFEREE,
Mr H. P. Hackney of Barnsley.

Nicholson lost the toss he so desperately wanted to win and was forced to attack the Kop in the first half but within moments Vale were on the move and in a goalmouth melee Mudie slipped the ball across to Smith only to see the winger fail to control his shot properly. Vale held their own spiritedly in these early minutes but Callaghan drew the best out of Hancock with a fast rising drive which the Vale keeper stylishly touched outside.

Sproson worked a neat move on the left before pushing the ball out to Richards and the centre-forward's low crossfield pass to Steele found its mark. The inside-forward drove hard and low from long range but Lawrence gathered easily.

MUDIE CLOSE

The Potteries club were certainly not looking the inferior outfit and in the 10th minute Mudie went the closest yet to scoring. The ball was flung across from the left by Richards and the inside-left adroitly flicked it goalwards with his right foot only to see it crawl past the post by inches.

It was ding-dong stuff. First Rawlings moved downfield to see a long shot bounce perilously close, than a low ground shot from Hunt was well taken by Hancock. In the 18th minute, Arrowsmith, so far well checked by Nicholson, crashed outside a good chance but within minutes, Stan Steele had twice drawn gasps from the Kop with grand efforts.

Mudie instigated the first with a pass which Steele took on the run to crash in a fine shot which Lawrence had difficulty in saving with one hand. Then the stocky inside-right belted in another drive which jumped uneasily from Lawrence's hands.

GREAT SPIRIT

Vale were warming to their attacking task with great spirit and from a Smith centre Richard's header was back-kicked for safety over the by-line by Byrne. There was peril for Liverpool in two successive flag-kicks which followed but both were cleared.

Up to this stage, Vale had certainly looked the more dangerous side and there was no doubt that Liverpool were getting an early taste of their traditional Cup fluency. But in the 32nd minute, Liverpool went within the merest fraction of taking the lead as Stevenson drove in a brilliant 30-yard left-footer which seemed to be veering into the corner of goal.

Hancock, however, threw himself across to push the ball against the post and the crowd gasped as it bounced away. Many thought it had in fact entered the net. When the pressure was on, Vale's defenders were working overtime. Thompson was a real power on Liverpool's left but another rising drive from the winger was blocked by the splendid Hancock.

Vale resumed the attack as Rowland dashed past Byrne to cross menacingly. The ball flew out to Smith on the far side of goal whose centre was flicked goalwards by Mudie but the effort was blocked. Rowland again showed his danger by working the ball inside from his flank to hit a low left-footer goalwards but again Lawrence was just able to clutch it on the ground.

This was a splendid first-half showing by Vale. The Potteries team had certainly not been consumed by the fire of Anfield and had for much of the half looked the more telling attackers. There had been thrills and spills at both ends but again Vale's defenders were showing their mettle.

HALFTIME:-
LIVERPOOL 0
PORT VALE 0

The second-half opened in the same stirring tempo of the first. Soon, Vale were attacking through Rowland who saw a swift left-footer clutched by Lawrence, then Richards had a high cross pushed over the by-line.

The next moments were Liverpool's. Arrowsmith rose to head a Callaghan cross close in but Hancock was there, then a St John header was fisted out by the keeper. But Vale returned to the attack swiftly. Smith and Mudie combined to send Richards away and the centre-forward's snap drive was pushed outside by Lawrence.

Then followed the game's closest call as Nicholson, cheered on voluminously by the crowd, moved down the middle. He pushed the ball out to Rowlands and the winger's turf-searing cross was missed by a fraction as Vale's skipper jumped in for the kill.

Of Vale's attackers, inside-forwards Mudie and Steele were playing prime hands. The little Scot had shown more than once the flicks and flourishes which stamp his play, while Steele was carving gaps for his colleagues with great assurance.

One lovely Vale move which cut across field and down to the right flank was hindered only because Rowland's cross was too quick for his inside colleague. Seconds later, Richards flung a ball into the area from the left and the crowd gasped as Mudie headed over.

Certainly Vale's followers were getting their money's worth. The Third Division team had surprised the home fans with their skill and enthusiasm and it looked at this stage as though a single goal would decide the game. Vale's role in this second-half was, supposedly, to defend the Kop against not only the Liverpool team but the verbal assault of the home crowd.

Misfortune struck the Vale seconds later as Mudie was fouled in a heavy tackle but he got back on to his feet after

treatment on the field. The injury, sustained in the 77th minute, seemed to affect the Scotsman badly, however, for he was hobbling painfully and Vale were deprived of his brilliant influence.

TEN MEN

Vale were now virtually playing with 10 men as Mudie stumbled painfully around the field at little more than walking pace. It was the harshest possible luck for a Vale team who had looked on top of this game but were now having to defend ruggedly.

In this stirring finale, the crowd's heart went out to the fine Vale side who had certainly performed better than their most ardent fan prophesised.

Gate receipts: £10,800.

25 January 1964

Ninety seconds rob Vale of their just deserts

Ninety seconds robbed gallant Port Vale of their chance of further Cup glory against the red-shirted stars of Liverpool at the finale of last nights 120 minute battle.

PORT VALE 1
LIVERPOOL 2

Vale, so near to a third meeting with the Cup favourites, were coasting confidently to a 1-1 draw when Liverpool cut through on the right only one and a half minutes from the completion of this thumping game. The ball was crossed into the middle and in the ping-pong scrimmage which followed, brilliant Peter Thompson volleyed in past a surprised Ken Hancock. It was a shot in a hundred and Vale were out of the Cup, but Liverpool will not easily forget the 210-minute battle which the valiant Potteries side put up in this momentous fourth round.

Another crack at the Liverpudlians would have been the only just reward for a Vale side who had revitalised themselves into an effective attacking outfit in the second half to equalise and force the game into 30 minutes of nail biting extra time.

It was the cruellest luck when Thompson lashed in his winner in the 199th-minute to produce a wholesale invasion of the Vale Park pitch by thousands of yelling Merseysiders. By any standards this was a match to remember. Over 42,000 fans jammed Vale Park but thousands more rushed the gates at the railway end.

CRUEL LUCK

Fans were carried away on stretchers with clockwork regularity – one Leek man died shortly afterwards and the events were climaxed as two Liverpool fans on top of the Railway stand roof crashed through the asbestos when Thompson hit his winner.

But what of the game? For 45 minutes Liverpool were the thoroughbred race horses against a team of earnest but ordinary toilers.

The Vale gradually found the measure of the opposition to produce the Cup form which has seen them through 25 battles in the last five seasons of the competition. When Albert Cheesebrough, playing in place of the injured Jackie Mudie, slipped in a slick equaliser in the 80th minute the Potteries team were well on top. The local side, moving forward in concert, had abandoned their air of desperation against skilled opposition to produce a pattern of play which had Liverpool back-wheeling and worried.

John Nicholson, Stan Steele, Ron Smith and Tim Rawlings removed their shin pads and rolled down their socks as a gesture of defiance. They fought to the 90 minute mark with bared shins – and thoroughly deserved their equality.

Only in the last gasp of extra time did Vale forfeit their Cup hopes...the second successive season they have suffered a 2-1 fourth round defeat at the hands of a First Division club. Vale's heroes on a night in which Liverpool showed their tempestuous class for 50 minutes of the encounter were again their splendid half-back trio.

Roy Sproson, playing with the sure, hard-tackling poise of his wing-half days of a decade ago, was with, Thompson, the game's outstanding figure.

It took fully 70 minutes for Vale's wingers to fulfil their purpose. When they did there were fireworks from Smith and Rowland which had Liverpool's chessboard-style defenders puffing.

With inside-right Stan Steele playing a fine deep game, Vale looked a force to be reckoned with as they moved in unison, building up their attacks intelligently. Earlier Vale's booted clearances had flown straight to opposition defenders – anywhere, in fact, but to their own loosely-formed attack. Liverpool were quick to take advantage, but Sproson, Rawlings and Nicholson steadied the home team, soldered the defence magnificently and prompted the later revival.

DANGER MAN

Liverpool's danger men were Thompson and international inside-right Roger Hunt. The inside-forward hinted at his class with a looping drive in the 29th minute which shaved the bar. And in the 35th minute Hunt darted in to intercept a punt from Byrne over the heads of Vale's defenders to slip the ball home.

St John had a close shot superbly saved by the Vale

keeper, but it was the last goal threat of the Liverpool attack for some time. Not so with Vale. In the 62nd minute Rowland cut inside to ram in a low left-footer which drew a fine on the ground stop from Lawrence.

In the 80th minute rampant Vale were rewarded. Rowland pushed the ball inside, Steele tapped it on and Cheesebrough slipped in a great opportunist goal. In to extra time they went and the huge crowd sensed the replay which justice demanded as the stalemate battle continued. But for Vale tragedy struck in the 119th minute Thompson let fly a brilliant desperate last chance shot which came off.

VALE:-
Hancock, Whalley, Wilson, Rawlings, Nicholson, Sproson, Rowland, Steele, Richards, Cheesebrough, Smith.

LIVERPOOL:-
Lawrence, Byrne, Moran, Milne, Yeats, Stevenson, Callaghan, Hunt, St John, Melia, Thompson.

REFEREE:-
Mr H. T. Hackney of Barnsley

Attendance: 42,179

28 January 1964

Goalkeeper Ken Hancock joined Vale in November 1958 from Stoke City. He played his debut match against Millwall and subsequently retained his place for the rest of the 1958 season. Hancock was a familiar face at Vale and finally left the club in 1964 when he joined Ipswich Town.

Old favourite at Vale "benefit"

At 7.30 p.m. today the clock will be turned back a decade as Port Vale's greatest Cup fighting team- the 1954 side who fought their way into the semi-final of the competition-take the field again.

The occasion is the twin benefit match for the only remaining member of that famous side still active in League soccer- wing-half Roy Sproson and his full-back colleague Selwyn Whalley. It should be an occasion to remember as the men who forged a League defensive record turn out on the Vale Park turf again to oppose the current team, goalkeeper Ray King, full-backs Stan Turner and Reg Potts, and half-backs Tom Cheadle and Sproson himself. Only right-half Albert Mullard is absent- he has left the district and has not been traced-and Stan Steele will be taking his place.

ONLY CHANGE

The attack which marched through eight successive Cup games to become the soccer phenomenon of the season shows only one change from the line-up which played in the Villa Park semi-final against West Bromwich- Albert Leake, player manager of Macclesfield Town, has a club fixture to fulfil. Only one member of tonight's front line was not a regular in the 1954 team-inside forward Derek Tomkinson. All the others right-winger Colin Askey, centre-forward Basil Hyward, inside-left Ken Griffiths and left-winger Dickie Cunliffe were automatic choices.

The 1954 side will take on the current team for a 45-minute exhibition. Then, after the interval, an All-Stars side, captained by Stan Matthews and including such names as Tom Finney and Joe Mercer, will take the field. Mercer, Manager of Aston Villa, is bringing along a number of his young stars to fill the team gaps if necessary, including centre-forward Tony Hateley and under-23 England international Alan Deakin.

Manager Freddie Steele – "if they are short I will probably turn out myself"- will be refereeing and announcements will be made on Vale's public address system so that fans are kept informed of team changes.

DEPUTIES

Vale will be fielding the side which beat Wrexham 5-0 on Saturday – with the exception of wing-halves Steele and Sproson. Harry Poole and Terry Miles will deputise.

Teams:-

PORT VALE (1964)
Hancock, Whalley, Wilson, Poole, Nicolson, Miles, Bingham, Cheesebrough, Richards, Porter, Smith.

PORT VALE (1954)
King, Turner, Potts, Steele, Cheadle, Hayward, Griffiths, Cunliffe, Sproson, Tomkinson, Askey.

27 April 1964

11,653 fans pay tribute to Sproson, Whalley

by J.B

Almost 12,000 fans paid their tribute to Port Vale's long serving wing-half Roy Sproson and full-back Selwyn Whalley at Vale park last night, 4,000 more than Port Vale's average attendance this season.

They filed through the turnstiles to a 45 minute match between Vale's current side and the all conquering 1954 Cup team, of which Sproson is the only remaining member still playing regularly in League football.

They applauded when an All-star team struck a more competitive note in the second half, to tax a full strength Vale team entertainingly.

Port Vale (1964) slimmer and benevolent in the tackling, were a shade too speedy for Port Vale (1954).

It did not prevent left-winger Dickie Cunliffe from wringing sentimental cheers from his old Railway Stand fans as he sped up and down the flank and did not stop the Lorne-street end supporters from willing their old centre-forward, Basil Hayward, to take centre-half, goalkeeper and ball into the net in one juggernaut rush.

REFEREE STEELE

And it did not deter that prince of centre-halves, Tom Cheadle, nor his doughty left-back colleague, Reg Potts from checking and checking well, the younger, newer members of Vale's staff.

Despite the efforts of referee Freddie Steele — a benevolent, almost immobile figure that refused to wander more than ten yards each side of the centre circle — Vale's current team won 2-0.

Referee Steele mistakenly blew his whistle for half time 15 minutes before schedule, but quickly corrected himself and diplomatically ordered a dropped ball.

Vale's second-half against and attack, which included Stan Matthews, Jackie Mudie, Billy Bingham and Aston Villa players Hateley and Burrows, was not so informal. In fact, it produced some rattling good soccer and a 3-3 draw.

The tall Hateley quickly showed he meant business with a header thudded into the back of the net with Ken Hancock helpless.

HIS PENALTY

Bingham and Mudie darted like dragonflies and Matthews worked on the tight flank with the delicate precision of an engineer.

It added to up to top entertainment and was crowned by a superb run from the goalkeeper Hancock in the final minute. Hancock dashed the length of the field and was particularly gratified when a mild tussle with the amicable Sproson produced a penalty. The goalkeeper promptly blasted the ball home for the first goal of his life.

A final word of praise for Aston Villa boss, Joe Mercer. He brought four of his first teamers to fill the gap and played himself. Results: Port Vale 1964 2 (Bingham, Cheesebrough), Port Vale 1954 0. Second-half: Port Vale 3 (Miles, Cheesebrough, Hancock), All Stars 3 (Hateley, Bingham, Burrows).

The Port Vale Chairman, Mr Tom Talbot, on behalf of his directors, thanks the public for their support of the match. He says it far exceeded expectations.

Waddington hat-trick saves the "Old Stars".

Bursting on to the playing scene last night, Stoke City Manager Tony Waddington scored a second-half hat-trick to save the game for Stoke's Old Stars in their meeting with the Supporters' Club XI on the Stoke City practice ground.

An exciting and entertaining tussle ended in a 4-4 draw.

The former Stoke Stars were 2-0 down at half-time and after 65 minutes were trailing 4-1.

It was then that Waddington stepped in to show the benefit of regular training with his players by swinging the game round in sensational fashion. Playing at inside-left he partnered Bert Mitchell.

He brought the score to 4-2 after 70 minutes with a right foot shot from 30 yards and in the 83rd minute made it 4-3.

SOLO EFFORT

Finally, in the closing minutes, he made it all square with a great solo effort.

The Supporters were two goals up after 15 minutes through their wingers Keith Dale, who is a member of Stoke City's office staff, and Dawson.

Frank Mountford reduced the gap early in the second-half but goals by Dale and Graham Johnson left the Old Stars apparently out of it, until Waddington's rescue act.

Stoke Old Stars.— Herod, Bourne, Graham (Stoke's trainer), Sellars, Mountford, Cairns, Brown (D), Kirkby, Caton, Waddington, Mitchell.

Supporters Club.— Bates, Bowden, Harrison, Garity, Yorke, Johnson (B), Dale, Johnson (G), Rushton, Meakin, Dawson.

28 April 1964

Port Vale sign Ron Andrew

Port Vale today signed Ron Andrew from Stoke City at a modest fee, believed to be about £3,000.

Andrew has had experience at centre-half and centre-forward, but he will be required by Vale as a partner for former Stoke colleague Ron Wilson at full-back, where he has performed soundly.

Andrew, who is 28, had been with Stoke 10 years, starting as a part-time professional. He joined the City from Ellesmere Port, the Cheshire County League club. For two seasons after the transfers of Ken Thomson to Middlesbrough he was Stoke's most regular choice at centre-half. He made 30 League appearances in 1959-60, 37 in 1960-61 and 35 in 1961-62. Two seasons ago he was succeeded by Eddie Stuart and since has made occasional first-team appearances at full-back.

Barry Hancock, Vale's transfer-listed reserve inside forward, travelled to Lincoln today for an interview with City Manager Bill Anderson. It is understood that Potteries-born Hancock will not be easily persuaded to leave the district. More likely is the transfer of reserve full-back Jim Watton to Doncaster. He is also to be interviewed by the club.

Vale's interest in both Peter Bullock and Leeds goalkeeper Brian Williamson has ceased. Manager Freddie Steele confirmed inquiry about the Birmingham and ex-Stoke player, but he was not pursuing the matter. Goalkeeper Williamson has re-signed for his club but Mr Steele said today that a keeper would definitely be signed before the end of the month.

24 June 1964

Vale's Stan Steele Re-signs

CREWE PRACTICE TOMORROW

Stan Steele, the last of Port Vale's pay rebels, re-signed today.

Steele is one of five players originally on monthly contracts who have now settled their differences with the club. Skipper John Nicholson, full-back Selwyn Whalley and reserves Melvin Machin and Mick Porter, now back in full training after his car accident injury, have all re-signed.

Tomorrow Vale play their third pre-season practice match with another club when they visit Gresty Road for a game with Crewe (kick-off 11 a.m.). The team have already had matches at Tranmere (0-0) and Wrexham (Vale won 2-0).

Explained Manager Freddie Steele: "We have plumped for pre-season away games because we felt this is where our weakness lay last season. The team have already played two full-scale practice games at Vale Park and the Gresty Road match will help them to get used to the atmosphere of a smaller ground."

DELIGHTED

In a pre-season message to Vale's supporters, the club Chairman, Mr Tom Talbot, says the Board are delighted the whole of the staff have now re-signed and the club are able to start the season in good heart and complete unity. While they were not making any wild promises, the club were quietly confident that they would have a reasonably successful season. They felt that the benefit of the new staff they engaged last season would be reaped this year. No stone would be left unturned to gain the ultimate goal of higher-grade football.

Vale have introduced a ticket innovation this season. They are offering a small allocation of 15-guinea tickets for seats in the Directors' box and already there has been a "quite reasonable" demand for them.

17 August 1964

Roy Sproson controlling the ball in a practice session at Vale Park. The Sprosons are a family who made playing football for Port Vale their profession. Elder brother Jess Sproson went through the junior ranks to make his debut for the Valiants in 1940 and eventually his son Phil also played 11 seasons for Vale. Roy Sproson went on to manage Port Vale in 1974 and stayed until 1977.

Showing his control skills, Clint Boulton takes possession of the ball. He made his debut for Vale in 1964, on Boxing Day, in a 3-0 home defeat to Hull City. Boulton was an essential player in Vale's Third Division promotion in the 1969-70 season.

Stanley Matthews's first signing for Port Vale is 15 year old Stoke schoolboy, John Hulme. Also pictured here is John's father Stanley Hulme and Jackie Mudie.

Jackie Mudie congratulates Sir Stanley Matthews on becoming General Manager at Port Vale in February 1965.

Chapter Five
1965-1970

With the collaboration between Jackie Mudie and Stanley Matthews Vale's initial future looked more hopeful. Matthews was a firm advocate of Vale's Youth Team policy and several notable figures emerged through these early signings.

By the culmination of the 1965-66 season Port Vale were back in the Fourth Division, in 19th place and only secured 39 points. In a decade the team had gone from FA semi-cup finalists to the bottom of the Fourth Division team. The team that Matthews had worked so hard to build up were having to be sold off, player by player and his good friend Jackie Mudie resigned from his position.

Disaster struck the Matthews administration in 1968 when the Football Association and the Football League started an inquiry into Vale's 'financial irregularities'. It came to light that illegal payments had been made to players and the club was fined £4,000 and excluded from the Football League.

Later in May of that same year Matthews resigned as Vale's manager but continued to support the innovative youth programme that he had instigated. Gordon Lee, ex-Aston Villa left-back, took on the manager role from Matthews. The club were re-elected into the Football League in June 1968.

By the end of the 1968-69 season Port Vale were 13th in the Fourth Division, 13 points behind the division leaders Doncaster. Under Gordon Lee's management Vale continued to improve although a financial cloud still overhung the club. One of the proposals made by the club was for Vale Park to be converted during the summer months into a speedway. This suggestion created so much hostility from local residents that even though the plans had been approved by the council, the consent was revoked and nothing came of the plans.

The 1969-70 season saw Port Vale finish fourth in the Fourth Division on 59 points. This was enough to secure promotion for the team back into the Third Division.

Stanley Matthews and Melvin Charles in training at Vale Park.

Expectant Vale Park crowd delighted by Sir Stan's new team

PORT VALE 1
COLCHESTER 0

Vale Park buzzed with excitement and speculation this afternoon as the new look Port Vale stepped out for the first time under the general managership of Sir Stanley Matthews

It was back to Fourth Division football for Port Vale and visitors Colchester United, managed by Neil Franklin, and the question on everybody's lips was whether Sir Stan could inspire a rapid return to the Third Division. Vale had three close season signings in the forward line, right-winger Smith and left-wing pair Morrison and Taylor.

Smith aged 20, and Bannister, who is 17, form one of the youngest winger pairings in Vale history; Roy Sproson and

Jackie Mudie were out after injury. Arthur Kaye, once the understudy at Blackpool of Stanley Matthews, was on Colchester's right-wing.

FAILED TEST

Inside forward Bobby Blackwood failed a fitness test and was replaced by Aitchison. Otherwise, the visitors were at full strength, with new signings Kaye Bell and Stratton and debutant Hornby.

PORT VALE:-
O'Neill, Lowe, Wilson, Poole, Nicholson, Miles, Smith, Bannister, Rowland, Morrison, Taylor. Substitute Boulton.

COLCHESTER UNITED:
Kennon, Forbes, Hall, Trevis, Loughton, Bell, Kaye, Aitchison, Stratton, Stark, Hornsby. Substitute, Jones.

REFEREE:
Mr D. W. Brady of Rotherham.

As an overture, the crowd were treated to a seven-a-side game by Vale's junior professionals. After heavy showers before the start the sun shone strongly

as Vale kicked off and there was a healthy sized crowd with more pouring onto the terraces. Danger threatened Colchester when Lowe, well supplied by Poole, advanced up the left wing, but with Rowland and Bannister waiting for the cross, the left-back put his centre into the side rigging.

LACKED POWER

Another well-tailored pass from Poole found Morrison unmarked in the penalty box but the inside-left's shot had not the power to beat goalkeeper Kennon, who smothered it on the line. A raking crossfield pass from Rowland set up a fine chance for Taylor, but after racing past full-back Forbes, the winger shot into the side of the net.

Kaye was doing intelligent mid-field work for the visitors but close tackling kept Colchester away from goal. Vale were playing short, along the carpet football that often had the visitors defence bewildered, but they had a tendency to make the extra pass that gave Colchester the extra chance to tighten up.

DESPERATE DIVE

A 30 yard ground shot by Miles from another precision pass from Poole almost took Kennon by surprise, but with a desperate dive across the line the goalkeeper kept the ball out. The zip of Vale's wingers was emphasised when Taylor again went past his opposite number in the penalty box, only to be obstructed.

From the free kick, Bannister shot first time but the outstretched boot of centre-half Loughton kept it out. Alternate showers and sunshine made conditions tricky for the goalkeepers but in the rare Colchester raids O'Neill's handling was competent.

Lowe was finding time to help his forwards and he unleashed a drive from 35 yards which drew a fine save from Kennon. It was a reflection on Colchester's lack of forward bite that Vale could afford to bring their defenders to the front line so often. A feature of play was the understanding between Miles and Taylor. Their short passing approach work was a delight.

FIRST OF SEASON

It was Taylor making a splendid debut who produced the brilliant headed pass that set up Vale's first goal in the 35th minute.

A Poole centre from the right wing floated across the goal and Taylor, leaping high by the far post, headed it back towards goal, where Bannister

came racing in to blaze the ball into the net from close range.

Minutes later, a fierce 25-yard drive by Rowland was spectacularly tipped over the bar by goalkeeper Kennon, who was having a busy afternoon. Vale had been cool in defence and imaginative in attack and this combination seemed too much for Colchester. It was a first half of quality and the crowd gave the players a well-deserved ovation as they left the field.

HALFTIME:- PORT VALE 1 COLCHESTER 0

Stark, Colchester's leading scorer last year, nearly put the visitors level immediately after the restart. Nicholson won a heading duel but the ball came back into the Vale penalty box and as Lowe mis-timed his tackle, the inside-left found the goal at his mercy. He shot wildly over the bar from an ideal position. At the other end, Poole drove well over the goal after Taylor had pulled the ball back from the left touchline. From a corner kick minutes later, Poole again shot over.

OVER BAR

Vale had lost some of their early precision but a move started by Morrison, whose penetrating

pass put Smith through on the left, ended with Bannister firing over the bar from a good position. Colchester were having a bigger ration of the attacking than in the first half and in the pouring rain, the sparkle seemed to have been washed from Vale's attack.

It was a comparatively dull period but Taylor enlightened it with a corkscrew run down the left before slipping the ball to Bannister, who had positioned himself intelligently but made a weak final shot, straight into Kennon's hands.

Rowland tried a snap shot along the ground and Kennon did well to dive and palm it for a corner. But there was a narrow escape for Vale when Kaye worked across the middle and gave Aitchison the opportunity for a quick shot at goal. With O'Neill beaten, Nicholson kicked off the line.

CROWD'S IDOL

Taylor, who had established himself as the idol of the crowd, had two more excellent rushes down the wing but the support he had found in the first half was not always forthcoming now. Lowe came up into the attack and gave a good pass to Smith on the right. The winger beat his man before sending over a perfect centre and Kennon just outreached Morrison to put the ball behind for a fruitless corner.

Trevis was working hard to get his forwards into gear as the minutes ticked away, but the visiting attack failed to knit and most of their efforts were individual ones. This was strikingly demonstrated when centre-forward Stratton took the ball along the left touchline and pulled it back towards the penalty spot. The move caught Vale's defence on the wrong foot but there was nobody there to collect the pass.

LEFT WINDED

The trainer was on the field for the first time when Bannister chased a pass from Miles into the penalty box. Kennon won the race but was winded in the collision. Vale ended on an attacking note and a fine effort by Rowland was put behind for a corner in brilliant style by Kennon, but the whistle blew before the kick could be taken. After the sparkling first half, the second was something of a disappointment but it was a performance of great promise and new boys Taylor, Smith and Morrison earned their laurels.

Vale attendance: 11,212

21 August 1965

Fourth Division action from 18 September 1965 and Vale's home game against Lincoln City. Vale were having a good start to the season having won five and drawn one of their first six games. They won this one too (3-0). Though they were in eleventh place they were only four points adrift of leaders Chester.

Scottish striker Mick Cullerton joined Port Vale in October 1965 and made his first team debut three months later in a defeat against Bradford City. In the 1966-67 season he became Vale's leading scorer.

Sir Stanley Matthews pictured with the 1965 Port Vale team.

Photographed here are the 1965 Vale Youth Team.

Sir Stanley Matthews with the 1967 Youth Team.

January 1966: Vale take to the sands at Lytham St Annes near
Blackpool as they prepare for their third round FA Cup clash against
Cardiff City.

Signed from Aberdeen, centre-forward John Cummings made only six first team appearances for Vale (in the 1965-66 season) and scored one goal. He then returned north of the border, signing for Ayr United.

A young Roddy Georgeson spent a relatively short interval at Vale from 1965-67. He joined the club as a forward from Scotland and appeared for 28 matches in which he scored 6 goals.

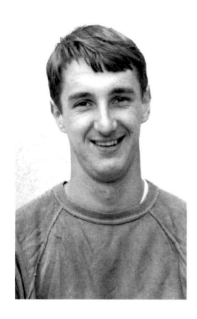

David Ikin made his debut goalkeeper in a 3-0 defeat at Aldershot on 12 February 1966. The parting of the ways came shortly after this for in May 1966 he was one of six players given a free transfer. Some of the other players up for transfer were: Terry Lowe, John Bostock, Barry Stubbs, David Mitchell and Tony Richards. Vale were also prepared to part in exchange for cash or players with wingers Roger Smith and Brian Taylor as well as inside-forward Melvin Machin.

Vale's fixture on 21 March 1966 was home game against fellow strugglers Hartlepool United. It ended in a goalless draw with Hartlepool being propped up by Rochdale and Lincoln City. Vale in 19th position were just three points ahead of Hartlepool; one behind Crewe Alexandra and Wrexham, and one ahead of

Vale gives six a free transfer: three on offer

Six Port Vale players were told today that they are to be given free transfers and three that they will be put on offer for transfer, although they are retained.

Above: Ron Wilson

The club have also agreed "reluctantly" to the transfer request of full-back Ron Wilson. Vale are prepared to part in exchange for cash or players with wingers Roger Smith and Brian Taylor, who were signed before the start of the current season, and local boy Melvin Machin, the 21-years-old inside forward who has been with no other club.

Free transfers are given to goalkeeper David Ikin, 20, full-back Terry Lowe, 24, John Bostock, 18 and Barry Stubbs, 18; "utility" player David Mitchell, 21, and centre-forward Tony Richards, 32.

RETAINED LIST

The 25-strong list of retained professionals is: Terry Alcock, Terry Bailey, Paul Bannister, Clinton Boulton, Michael Cullerton, Alex Donald, Roddy Georgeson, Jimmy Hill, John James, Alan Johnson, Gordon Logan, Malcolm MacKenzie, Terry Miles, Jackie Mudie, Jimmy O'Neill, Harry Poole, John Richie, John Rowland, Stuart Sharratt, Roy Sproson, Roger Smith, Melvin Machin, Brian Taylor, David Tunstall and Ron Wilson.

Player-Manager Jackie Mudie said today that Vale would be endeavouring in the close season to sign one or two new players. "The aim is to bring more power to the attack," he added. "We will be studying the retained lists of other League clubs and by this I do not necessarily mean that we will only go for players on free transfer. We may be able to spend some money, especially with the saving in our wages bill brought about by our list."

There are no real surprises in the list, although a few eyebrows may be raised over the decision to put Machin on offer.

COST £3,000

The club can give no indication of what they hope to get for Brian Taylor, but they paid £3,000 when they signed him from Shrewsbury. Smith came from Walsall on a free transfer.

Former Birmingham City player Tony Richards, who was signed from Walsall for £9,000 in the 1962-63 season, almost went to Nuneaton Borough in February this year but refused the Southern League club's terms after Vale had offered him on a free transfer. During his career with Vale he has suffered from a bad knee injury and last season was able to make only one appearance, although he has been in the team 15 times this term and scored six goals.

Ron Wilson, the 24-years-old Edinburgh born defender, joined Vale from Stoke City, together with Jackie Mudie in a £12,000 "package deal" in November, 1963. He was playing with a local junior side, Musselburgh Wanderers, before joining Stoke. He made a written transfer request two weeks ago after losing his first team place.

RELUCTANT

Mr Mudie said today: "We have agreed to put Ron on offer with great reluctance, but we feel that if he is unhappy it would be unfair to keep him here."

Vale reserve, who visit Atherstone tonight in their last fixture of the season, include Taylor, Richards, Machin and Mitchell. The team will be: McNulty, Mitchell, Logan, Johnson, Dickson, Miles, MacKenzie, Machin, Richards, Tunstall, Taylor.

Kick-off 7.30.

Sir Stanley Matthews today set off on his six weeks tour of South Africa, flying by way of Manchester, London, Paris and Johannesburg. He will play in six matches for the Wanderers of Joannesburg. Lady Matthews is accompanying him.

12 June 1966

Left-winger Michael Mahon was one of Vale's recruits from amateur football for the start of the 1966-67 season. Mahon, a 21 year old England amateur was about to start his final year at Loughborough College where he was studying for a teaching certificate. He said "I hope to put in as many appearances with Vale as my studies permit. At the moment there's a snag about Saturday morning lectures which could keep me away from games more than three hours car-drive from college. Being at college also means I will have to do my training by myself in the evening." No less than 26 League clubs had attempted to sign Mahon, so why Port Vale? In a brief interview Mahon explains his reasoning for going to Vale: "The whole set up is as good as anything in the First Division, including the terms. Sir Stan and Jack Mudie are two gentlemen very much aware of players' needs. You are made to feel at home straight away and nothing is too much trouble. They treat you with respect and consideration – It's something you don't find too often."

Port Vale are hoping to reap the dividends of their youth policy this season

Can Port Vale build successfully on the firm foundations of their youth policy, which were implanted so swiftly and comprehensively last season? The answer could well decide the future of the club.

In a season when League success was elusive and money in short supply, supporters were able to peer through the gloom and see that the seeds of success were being sown. The coming season could see a good harvest, if not a golden one. The process of blooding Vale's young discoveries last term was inevitably accompanied by set-backs, but for the coming campaign the teenagers will be richer for the experience.

"These boys have had a taste of tough, Fourth Division football and it will have done them a world of good," says Player-Manager Jackie Mudie. "This year we intend to play a young side, averaging 20 or less, and we think we can do well."

Last season, he points out, the club were going through the birth pangs of the youth policy and success was never really expected. "But now we are a more settled outfit altogether," he says. "Most of the experimenting has been done. We know players' capabilities and weaknesses. We can start the season on a firm footing."

So supporters can expect to see much more of teenagers like Georgeson, Cullerton, Donald and MacKenzie. The youthful half-back line of James, Alcock and Boulton has already shown such authority that the term "young hopefuls" will never apply to them again. They are men among men, as Sir Stanley Matthews puts it.

Vale's side will not lack experience. Senior players like Sproson, Poole and Miles, forwards with the skill and flair of Jimmy Hill and John Rowland, will bring a big ration of know-how to the team. There is, too, the distinguished trio of tough North Eastern players who reached the amateur heights before joining Vale. John Ritchie has already proved himself a rugged, intelligent man capable of taking any position, and Jimmy Goodfellow and Michael Mahon, who will be in their first season, promise an abundance of craft in the front line.

BIG NEED

As well as craft, the front line will need punch and there is no sidestepping the issue at Vale Park. "We must improve our marksmanship," says Mr Mudie. "Our financial position is well known, but I assure supporters that we will do all we can to bring new fire to the forward line."

Three of last season's regular forwards have gone, Machin to Gillingham, Richards to Nuneaton and Smith to Walsall. Paul Bannister is recovering well from a broken leg and could make a good come back during the season and winger Brian Taylor, who has been put on the transfer list, might react by stepping up his performances.

Goodfellow, Mahon, Hill and one of the young Scots could well be worked into a blend to produce the scoring opportunities Rowland is capable of taking. Vale's defence has few weak links. Stuart Sharratt, who took over from Jimmy O'Neill last season should improve his already impressive goalkeeping reputation in only his second season as a League player.

Vale have a large, ever-growing pool of young players to draw from, and every player at Vale Park be he 15 or 35 knows there will be a first team place for him if he merits it. Intensive scouting in the North East and Scotland will continue and eyes will be turned over the border to watch the progress of Broxburn Athletic, the Scottish junior league club taken over as a Vale "nursery."

NEW GROUND

Another new ground for Vale this season will be at Leek Town, where training will take place and "A" team matches staged. Together with the excellent Unity-avenue, Sneyd Green pitch and the facilities open to Vale at R.A.F. Tern Hill, this represents for the club an admirable choice of venues. But it is to Vale Park, lovingly manicured to perfect condition by new groundsman Dennis Dawson, that the most eager glances will be directed on August 20th when Southport provide the opposition in the first match of a fascinating season. It will be the firm hope of every supporter that among the spectators will be Sir Stanley Matthews.

4 August 1966

20 August and Vale are at home to Southport in the first game of the 1966-67 season. Vale won 2-1, which left them as joint holders of the second slot with Crewe Alexandra, and Southend United. Bradford Park Avenue were enjoying being at the top following their 4-1 win at home against Notts County.

Jimmy Goodfellow was Vale's second signing for the 1966-67 season. Along with Michael Mahon, Jimmy was also a member of the England amateur squad and had also won an FA Amateur Cup winners' medal with Crook Town.

Pictured in the changing rooms, from left to right: Terry Miles, Jimmy Goodfellow, Stuart Chapman and Terry Alcock. Mid-fielder, Jimmy Goodfellow originally played for Crook Town and Bishop Auckland before joining Port Vale. He made his debut for the Valiants against Southport in August 1966. Eventually Goodfellow became assistant manager and then manager of Cardiff City. Another mid-fielder pictured here is Stuart Chapman, he joined Vale as an amateur in June 1966. He made his debut against Lincoln City in 1967 but was unable to make a regular place on the team. He was given a free transfer in May 1970 and went on to become player-coach for Rocester.

Right-back Gordon Logan (front) in training at Vale Park. Logan became a Scotland youth international and graduated through Vale's juniors to sign 'pro' in March 1967. He did not secure a place in the first team and was given a free transfer in May 1970.

6 May 1967 and Vale's 42nd League fixture of the season was a home game against Hartlepool United. Pictured here is Roddy Georgeson heading the ball away from the Hartlepool players. The match ended in a goalless draw, enough to keep Hartlepool in seventh place and Vale in twelfth.

Roy Sproson (left) and Malcolm Bailey pictured here in Vale Park's changing rooms. Right-half Malcolm Bailey graduated through Vale's juniors and signed professional in May 1967. He failed to gain a regular place on the team and was given a free transfer in May 1970.

Vale are at home to Chester on 22 August 1967 in the first round of the League Cup. Vale won 3-0; some of the other results that day were Bournemouth 1 Watford 1; Leyton Orient 1 Gillingham 1; Middlesbrough 4 Barnsley 1; Swindon Town 1 Newport County 1; Torquay United 0 Exeter City 0; Walsall 4 Shrewsbury Town 2. By the way the ball wasn't on the original picture – it was added by the Sentinel for effect.

Pictured here at Vale Park, from left to right are: Terry Alcock (who played both right-back and centre-half in his career at Vale); Roy Sproson (known affectionately as 'Mr Loyalty' for his dedication and long-service to the club) and Harry Poole (who scored 79 goals during his time at Port Vale).

Wilkinson, Lawton in England youth trials

Steve Wilkinson, 16-years-old Stoke City centre-forward, and Port Vale goalkeeper Mike Lawton, 17 have been chosen for the first series of England Youth international trials at Cleethorpes from September 25th to 27th. Wilkinson, who joined Stoke straight from St Thomas's R.C. School, has represented Stoke-on-Trent Boys. He made 10 Central League appearances last season and played on the right-wing against Albion Reserves last week.

Lawton, who hails from Liverpool, joined Port Vale as an apprentice Professional straight from school at 15. Last season Mike Cullerton and Billy McNulty gained Scottish Youth caps and John James had England Youth trials.

7 September 1967

Members of the 1967-68 Port Vale team. Back row, from left to right: Terry Miles, Harry Poole, (unknown), Roy Chapman, Stuart Sherratt, John James, Gordon Logan, Ronnie Wilson. Middle row: Dave McClelland, Mick Morris, Roy Sproson, Clint Boulton, Mick Cullerton. Front: Mike Mahon and Jimmy Goodfellow.

Vale at home to Chester at a snow-kissed Vale Park for the first round of the FA Cup. Alas this wasn't to be one of Vale's better cup runs. In fact they went down and out by two goals to one. 9 December 1967.

Left: Mike Cullerton was a skilful forward who joined Vale in October 1965. His debut against Bradford City in 1966 resulted in a 2-0 defeat. Cullerton finished the 1966-67 season as Vale's top scorer. Cullerton later returned to Vale as a player and then became commercial manager in 1982. He remained in this position from 1982-1985 when he left to take up the same position at Stoke City.

Right: Roddy Georgeson was born in 1948 in Shubra, Egypt. He joined Vale on trial in October 1965. He made his debut for Vale in the same match as Mike Cullerton against Bradford. Georgeson appeared sporadically for Vale until July 1967 when he was granted a release after failing to agree terms with the club.

Heading the ball is Bobby Gough and running towards him to give him support is John James. Bobby Gough played for Walsall before joining Vale in 1968. He made his debut for Vale against Chesterfield in a 3-1 defeat and was a member of the 1969-70 Fourth Division promotion side. Defender and striker, John James came through the junior ranks at Vale and made his debut for the first team in 1966. James became Vale's top scorer in the 1969-70 season but after injury and two cartilage operations, he was eventually sold on to Chester in 1973 for £5,000.

Left to right: Dave McClelland, Mick Morris and Roy Sproson in August 1967. McClelland was a right-winger for Bishop Auckland, he signed for Vale after a trial in August 1967. He failed to gain a regular place on the team and was given a free transfer in April 1968.

Paying homage to Roy Sproson as he walks onto the pitch. From left to right: John Brodie, Bobby Gough, Brian Horton, Sam Morgan, Mick Morris, Robert Peyton. Roy Sproson played an amazing 836 League and Cup appearances between November 1950 and May 1972. He played his last game for Vale in 1972 against Rotherham United, he was 41 years old. He remained with Vale as a coach and also spent time as the Valiants' manager.

Seen here at Vale Park are Roy Chapman (left) and Sir Stanley Matthews. Stanley Matthews took over as Manager for Port Vale from Jackie Mudie. Matthews remained in this role from 1967-1968.

Pictured are the members of the International XI who met a Port Vale side for a testimonial match at Vale Park in 1967. In front from left to right: Harry Poole, Sir Stanley Matthews and Terry Miles. Stood behind from left to right: Alcock, James, Nichols, Chapman, Allen, O'Neill, Barnes, Franklin, Ritchie and Lofthouse.

Expulsion for Port Vale?

THE CHARGES

Charges faced by the Vale were;-

1) That a number of registered amateurs and associate school boys had received a regular weekly wage in contravention of FA Rule 25 (A).
2) That associate schoolboys had played for the club in contravention of FA Rule 33 and League Regulation 48.
3) That extra bonuses had been offered in contravention of League Cup Rule 16 to players to beat Chester F.C. in the League Cup-tie played on August 21 1967.
4) That a signing bonus and other payments had been paid to J. Ritchie on the 6 May, 1967, in contravention of Football League Regulations 42.
5) That signing on bonuses of £300 and £200 had been paid to C. W. Boulton and G. T. Logan respectively in contravention of Football League regulation 42.
6) That a director of Port Vale F.C. had made many gifts to young players, and the club was aware of this

as minuted 14 January 1966, which would appear contrary to FA Rule 25 (A).

CLUB "SHOCKED AND APPALLED" AT PENALTIES

Port Vale are "shocked and appalled" at the severity of the penalties imposed by the Football Association.

After consultations at the club offices the Vice-Chairman, Mr Arthur McPherson issued a statement saying:

"We are shocked and appalled at the severity of the findings of the inquiry. We did not think they would be as severe as this." Mr McPherson said: "Sir Stanley Matthews feels, quite justifiably, after having been a sporting ambassador of this country for over 30 years, the deepest concern at the findings. At the moment, there is no question of his resignation and he has given no indication that this is what he wishes to do."

Asked about the prospect of playing non-league football, the Vice-Chairman said:

"That is a possibility but, please God, it does not happen. We have been used to fighting at Vale Park and will keep on fighting.

STILL HOPE

"We have not lost hope, but obviously I cannot discuss anything like this at the moment because we do not know the Football League findings."

Asked about the question of an appeal, Mr McPherson said: "The decision regarding appeal will be considered at a later meeting."

Another director, Mr Fred Burgess said: "I am shocked and appalled at the findings. They are absolutely too severe altogether. This is a sad day for the club and everyone connected with it."

FIRST CENSURE FOR SIR STANLEY

Today's censure on Sir Stanley is the first ever passed on England's greatest right-winger. He was never reported during the whole of his playing career, which stretched from 1932 to 1965.

He was the biggest box-office draw the game has known and he received a knighthood in the New Year Honours List of

1965. Prince Philip paid this tribute to him on the occasion of his official farewell match at Stoke that year: "No-one can estimate the immense contributions which Stanley Matthews has made to football and a good sportsmanship in every part of the world. He has become a legend in his own time, which is a distinction reserved for only really great men."

Sir Stanley became Vale's General Manager in July 1965, a few months after his memorable testimonial match. He had crowned an incomparable career by reviving Stoke City and helping them to regain First Division status. Then, instead of retiring from the scene, he plunged himself into the battle to do for Fourth Division Port Vale what he had achieved as a player for Stoke City.

Now all his efforts have ended in the tragedy of the commission of inquiry.

Mr Norman Jones, the club Secretary, began with Vale in an honorary capacity in 1941-42, and in 1949 was appointed the full-time Secretary. He was then one of the youngest officials in the League.

IS THIS JUSTICE?

The "Sentinel" says:-

Port Vale's fate at the hands of the FA and Football League Joint Commission will revive again then system of justice in the game. There is no comparison between this system and that on which courts of law are based.

FA and League officials are both judge and jury, and the accused party has no right to be legally represented. Hearings are held behind closed doors and no opportunity is given for the case for the defence to be reported.

There is a wide-spread opinion among football supporters that penalties are out of proportion to the seriousness of the offences. Crushing blows of the kind dealt to Port Vale and to Peterborough United could well put out of business clubs who are already struggling to stay afloat financially.

22 February 1968

Free transfer for eight Port Vale players

Mick Morris, 23-years-old utility forward, is one of eight players given a free transfer by Port Vale.

Morris, recalled to the first-team for the last League game at Lincoln, joined Vale from Oxford United on a free transfer last summer, and impressed Manchester City Manager Joe Mercer in one home game against Luton Town.

Also on the "free" list are wing-halves Terry Miles and Harry Poole, who shared a joint testimonial at the beginning of the season for their 15 years' service. Other men on the list are: Scottish youth international goalkeeper Bill McNulty, who requested his release to return to Scotland; goalkeeper Mike Lawton; wing-half Melvin Lintern; and wingers Alex Donald and Malcolm Mackenzie.

RETAINED

Roy Sproson, long-serving defender, figures on the retained list of 24 at the age of 37. Also retained is forward Paul Bannister, who has twice broken his leg. Other players retained are:- Asprey, Boulton, Roy Chapman, Cullerton, James, Logan Gibbon, Goodfellow, Mahon, Sharratt, Sproson, Wilson, Bailey, Baker, Aleksic, Broomhall S. Chapman, McLaren, Mountford, Buckley, Tait, Miller, Lees, Bannister.

Centre-half Bill Asprey leaves tomorrow with a party including Stoke's George Eastham for a coaching trip to Zambia. Asprey, an FA coach, paid a similar visit to Rhodesia last summer.

12 May 1968

Vale back in again – only nine against (Shipman warns of snap inspections)

PORT VALE WERE READMITTED TO THE FOOTBALL LEAGUE BY 40 VOTES TO NINE AT THE ANNUAL MEETING OF THE LEAGUE IN LONDON TODAY

Vale were expelled at the end of the season and fined a total of £4,000 by a Football Association and Football League joint commission of inquiry for breaches of rules, mainly concerning illegal payments.

Yesterday Vale were assured of receiving the four votes cast by the Third and Fourth Division clubs, who are associate members of the league, so that the nine clubs who voted against them belong to the First and Second Divisions. Most of the opposition stemmed from the feeling that Peterborough United, similarly found guilty by a commission of inquiry, were treated harshly in comparison by being relegated to the Fourth Division when they had a chance to win promotion from the Third Division.

Re-election means that Vale's only effective punishment was the fines, which many people considered were harsh, but the League clubs were probably influenced by the fact that Vale will have considerable changes in administration next season, with a new Chairman, new Directors and a new manager-coach.

"I would like to thank all clubs concerned for voting us back," said Mr Arthur McPherson, the club's Chairman. "It has been like waiting for an operation."

LEARNED LESSON

Mr McPherson added: "Nothing is certain in football, and we could never breath easily until this vote of confidence by the clubs. We have learned our lesson, and I am sure we are going to progress now. We have a young enthusiastic manager, and we intend to move forward and forget this nightmare experience."

With General Manager Sir Stanley Matthews playing football in Canada and new Manager Gordon Lee on holiday, the Vale Chairman was accompanied at the meeting by Secretary Norman Jones and Director Don Ratcliffe.

One of the first acts by the Vale Chairman was to thank Stoke City Chairman Mr Albert Henshall, for assisting them in the campaign to give them a favourable recommendation to first and second division clubs.

LONG CAMPAIGN

The result ends a long campaign by Mr McPherson who had circulated the member club about reasons the club's amenities and reasons for continuing in membership after their shattering expulsion earlier this year.

Bradford, Workington, Chester and York also won re-election with plenty to spare, and, as expected, there was no real desire for change. But spectators will welcome a decision that players names, plus substitutes, must now be with the referee at least half an hour before the start.

FINANCIAL CRISIS

Mr Len Shipman, President of the League, gave a warning that snap inspections of a selected number of clubs' books would be made each season. Mr Shipman said: "As a result of the investigations of Peterborough and Port Vale, the Management Committee have decided that the present trend in football is leading the game into a situation which can only result in financial crisis for many clubs and serious damage to the League. They feel that in the changing circumstances of free negotiations, due regard is not being paid as it should be to the regulations of the Football League.

DEFERRED TERMS

"Some time ago a provision was included in Regulation 35 for the management Committee to arrange for an inspection of clubs' books, and it is the intention of the Management Committee, starting from the next season, to carry out snap inspections of a selected number of clubs' books each season."

Mr Shipman also voiced the Management Committee's concern about the increasing number of clubs who secure the transfer of a player on deferred terms and fail to honour their agreement with the transferring club on that date.

8 June 1968

Vale's new chief ready to meet big challenge

Bob Mountford came to Port Vale as part of the clubs youth development programme. He eventually left the Valiants' to play for Rochdale in 1975.

Gordon Lee, enthusiastic young man of the moment at Vale Park, could have settled for a quiet obscure existence at Shrewsbury. Instead he has taken up one of Soccer's biggest challenges to make people sit up and take notice of Port Vale, writes PETER HEWITT.

Already he is having a impact on the playing and training staff with his obvious sincerity and dedication. For he has imbued everyone with his own brand of enthusiasm for soccer.

"We must all talk about the game," he tells his men. "Think about what you are doing, discuss the game with yourselves, me or anyone. But let's all go over our games in future."

So Vale suddenly found themselves talking and expressing their views after their recent home defeat to Second Division Sheffield United.

Lee, honest, forthright and putting his cards on the table, said:

"People say we want new men. All right, fair enough. But I cannot pick up a cheque book and go out and sign them. It takes money and we just haven't got it. It will take time. What we must do here is to learn from our mistakes. And believe me we learned a heck of a lot from that Sheffield match. Everyone was invited to give his views. We held them in the first half and I thought we were the better side. So we were on the right lines. In the second half we fell down. There was a reason for it and now I think everyone knows why we fell down. I think we showed the public just how good and how bad we can be in that United match. You might say that they were virtually a First Division side so they ought to beat us. I do not accept that view. No team should be allowed to come to Vale Park and win without some logical explanation."

So gradually Manager Lee, talking, coaching, reasoning,

eating and sleeping soccer, is making his players more football conscious. The past is gone. And Gordon Lee means the future to herald a brighter dawn. The new look Vale Board, under Chairman Mr Arthur McPherson, were immediately impressed with Mr Lee's intense desire to prove himself as a manager. So he gained the vote in preference to more experienced men who had failed at other clubs.

Gordon Lee has yet to fail, which gives him a head start over almost everyone else at Vale after last season's disastrous time.

"I had to try this challenge," he said. "I did not want to hang around with one club all my life settling for a cushy number and seeing everyone else getting on in the game."

Ironically, jus a few weeks after taking the plunge with Vale, Shrewsbury were advertising for a manager-coach when Arthur Rowley settled for an equally insecure existence at Bramall Lane. But Mr Lee has no regrets, for Vale have given him his big chance and he means to make something of it. So far Mr Lee has not spared himself. He has supervised the coaching and training and then somehow found time for the hundred and one jobs that make up a Soccer manager's life.

So Vale's destiny at the moment lies in the hands of Gordon Lee and last season's senior squad minus Harry Poole and Terry Miles, but strengthened by ex-Tranmere men, Johnny King and Graham Williams. Wing-half King takes over the captaincy from loyal Roy Sproson, who intends to give up his 18-year professional career at Vale Park at the end of the season.

These then are the newcomers, joining Vale as professionals dedicated to giving a little more success to Burslem's Soccer population. How does Mr Lee regard his role as a manager?

"There is, of course, extra responsibility. What counts now is winning matches. By how many goals is not so important but I wouldn't have missed the chance for the world. We have a loyal bunch of supporters here. At Shrewsbury we were in the promotion race to the Second Division for most last season and still the crowd was on the 6,000 mark. Vale had over 3,000 for a friendly, so I am sure we can double that with reasonable success and that's what I mean to give them."

In addition to the new men, Vale still have the dependable Roy Chapman upfront after striking 25 goals last season. He needs more support this time, for inevitably he will be

a marked man as opponents study his record.

The difference between the top and bottom in the Fourth Division is small. If men like Mick Morris or Mick Cullerton can provide the necessary gaol support in attack then Vale could be climbing up the table. It would be optimistic to bracket Vale in the promotion possibles on the strength of two signings. What Vale have to do is to prove that the reprieve given to them by member clubs has not been displaced and that a spring-board is under construction in preparation for the eventful jump up.

Port Vale, the club that nearly died of shame, is alive and bursting with zeal, spirit and warmth. The challenge is tremendous, but the will to succeed is already in the club.

7 August 1968

Free tranfers for five Port Vale players

Port Vale Manager Gordon Lee has finished his first season in office by giving five players free transfers when his retained list was finally announced today.

Heading the list are Roy Chapman, top scorer in his two seasons with Vale, and former amateur internationals Michael Mahon and Jimmy Goodfellow, who both joined Vale from the North-East three seasons ago. Chapman joined Chester today.

Former Welsh international winger Graham Williams, who made Vale his sixth League club when signing on a free transfer from Tranmere at the end of last season, is not retained. And neither is Mick Cullerton, a former Scottish youth international, who two seasons ago was being hailed as Vale's most valuable property.

Goalkeeper Stuart Sharratt, who turned down a reported £15,000 transfer to Second Division Huddersfield two seasons ago, has accepted part-time terms which means that Vale will also release Milija Aleksic, who has been awaiting a decision on his future since finishing his apprenticeship last month.

---

12 FULL-TIME

Vale have therefore retained 12 full-time professionals, signed Stuart Chapman and kept Bob Mountford and Stephen Tait as apprentices. Of the retained players John James has been granted a transfer at his own request.

Players retained are: Bailey, Ball, Boulton, Stuart Chapman, Gough, Green, James, King, Logan, McLaren, Morris, Sharratt (part-time), Sproson, Wilson. Apprentices; Mountford, Tait.

Roy Chapman was released from his present contract, but offered revised terms. These Chapman found unacceptable, and today he signed for Chester, as expected.

Workington and Tranmere could be two clubs interested in winger Mahon, a qualified schoolteacher, who signed full-time for Vale on completing his studies at Loughborough College, where he won amateur caps. Mahon previously played for Newcastle United, making one Second Division appearance against Middlesbrough and scoring the winning goal in Newcastle's 4-3 victory. In his three seasons with Vale, Mahon made 96 League and Cup appearances, and scored 23 goals. On his day he hass looked a fine winger, but has been let down by inconsistency.

CLOSE DECISION

Goodfellow was signed from famous amateur Bishop Auckland. He made 85 first-team appearances for Vale and scored nine goals. Mr Lee says that Goodfellow was a "border-line case."

Many may consider the case of Cullerton a tragedy. In his first season of League Soccer as a 17-year-old, he was Vale's top scorer with 12 goals. Last season he hit nine, but after scoring only once in 22 games this term, Cullerton was left out of the Vale side and spent the last two months of the season on loan to Chester.

Williams came to Vale Park as one of Gordon Lee's first signings, but also scored only once in 23 League and Cup games and faded out in the second half of the season, apart from an obviously sentimental farewell appearance against Wrexham, his home town club. Commenting on his list Mr Lee said: "It was a hard decision, knowing that the players had given me their best, but in some cases I was looking for a little more and I have had to create the room for improvement. Now I am looking for four players, three forwards and a defender.

23 June 1969

Pictured here with the Port Vale squad from left to right are: Len Cliff (Director), Arthur McPherson (Chairman) and Gordon Lee (Manager). For Gordon Lee Port Vale was the first club where he held a managerial capacity, he went on to lead the team to promotion to the Third Division in the 1969-70 season.